EARLY RESPONSES TO *THE CORRESPONDENCE*

"Questions that occurred to me as I read this brilliant, baffling book: What the hell is this? *Who* the hell is this? Is this poetry? How can that sentence be so good? Can I steal that later? In 130 pages, J. D. Daniels shows you just about everything great prose can do. Books like this are why I read."
—Tom Bissell, author of *Apostle*

"Through the speed and shocking cuts of his prose, J. D. Daniels shows us what it is to be a writer now. Each of these six letters is a modern expression of Baudelaire's tortured prayer: 'O Lord God grant me the grace to produce a few good verses, which shall prove to myself that I am not the lowest of men, that I am not inferior to those whom I despise.'"
—Michael Clune, author of *Gamelife*

"Masculinity as vulnerable, smelly smackdown, personal failure as syntactic delight: In this volatile, brilliant collection, J. D. Daniels recollects in not-quite tranquillity a series of synesthesiac rearrangements of the self. The riveting swerves of his sentences and of his geographic and spiritual wanderings will make you keep asking what 'here' might be. These essays pay tribute to 'the world . . . our common property.'" —Lisa Cohen, author of *All We Know*

"What a nutjob! Increasingly these three words constitute my highest praise for—almost my ideal of—a writer, and in this regard J. D. Daniels takes the biscuit. I love the way he throws out everything, both in the sense of throwing it all at us, and the opposite: discarding everything that might be deemed necessary to the seemly construction of narrative. So *The Correspondence* gives us the best of both worlds."

—Geoff Dyer, author of *White Sands*

"J. D. Daniels's *The Correspondence* is an epic in fragments: masterly, comic, wise, daring. It is a book for everyone, from Kentucky to Cambridge to Kathmandu, though as a reader you may feel that Daniels is trafficking in secrets meant for you alone. It is occult. It is so strong, it will melt the books on the shelves around it. This is a book that will become a legend, introducing one of the very best writers in the country. If I could thrust it into every true reader's hands, I would."

—Mark Greif, author of *Against Everything*

"J. D. Daniels sees what others don't, feels what others won't, and writes what others can't. He is a blazing virtuoso of the English sentence, an oracle with a vulnerable and willing heart, and he has produced a shockingly perfect book."

—Sarah Manguso, author of *300 Arguments*

THE CORRESPONDENCE

THE

CORRESPONDENCE

J. D. DANIELS

Farrar, Straus and Giroux   *New York*

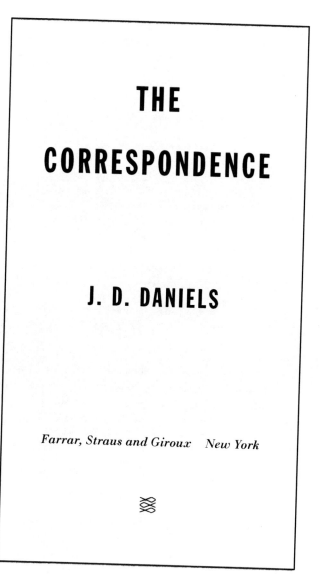

Farrar, Straus and Giroux
175 Varick Street, New York 10014

Published in 2017 by Farrar, Straus and Giroux
First paperback edition, 2018

The Library of Congress has cataloged the
hardcover edition as follows:
Names: Daniels, J. D., 1974– author.
Title: The correspondence / J. D. Daniels.
Description: New York : Farrar, Straus and Giroux, 2017.
Identifiers: LCCN 2016017824| ISBN 9780374535940
(hardback) | ISBN 9780374714666 (Ebook)
Subjects: | BISAC: LITERARY COLLECTIONS / Essays.
Classification: LCC AC8.5 .D26 2017 | DDC 814.6—dc23
LC record available at https://lccn.loc.gov/2016017824

Paperback ISBN: 978-0-374-53742-5

Designed by Jonathan D. Lippincott

Our books may be purchased in bulk for promotional,
educational, or business use. Please contact your local
bookseller or the Macmillan Corporate and Premium Sales
Department at 1-800-221-7945, extension 5442, or by e-mail at
MacmillanSpecialMarkets@macmillan.com.

www.fsgbooks.com
www.twitter.com/fsgbooks • www.facebook.com/fsgbooks

P1

This book is mainly nonfiction. "Letter from Cambridge,"
"Letter from Majorca," "Letter from Kentucky," and
"Letter from the Primal Horde" were written as essays
and should be read as such. "Letter from Level Four" and
"Letter from Devils Tower" were written as short stories
and do not describe real people or events. All of these
letters first appeared in *The Paris Review*.

for my father and my mother

and for SK

Maybe the real novel is letters to you.
—William S. Burroughs

CONTENTS

LETTER FROM CAMBRIDGE

A couple of years ago I joined one of those clubs where they teach you how to knock the shit out of other people. The first lesson is how to get the shit knocked out of yourself. The first lesson is all there is. It lasts between eighty and a hundred years, depending on your initial shit content.

✳

There is no diamond as precious as a tooth, so I shoved a boil-and-bite mouthpiece into my backpack with my cup and jockstrap before I headed for Allston to begin studying Brazilian jiu-jitsu. It was 5:00 a.m. on a January morning in 2008.

The gym was under a laundromat and it smelled like a sweat sock. I looked around and saw an octagonal cage with its door hanging open, a boxing ring, four heavy bags, kettle bells, medicine balls, a rowing machine, interlocking mats on the floor, and a sign in the bathroom that said HEY GENIUS, DO NOT PUT PAPER TOWELS IN THE TOILET.

I signed a standard waiver promising not to sue the management in the extremely probable event of my incurring an injury. I was thirty-three years old, five-ten, one-sixty.

We ran laps and did five hundred sit-ups, a hundred of this, a hundred of that. Then Big Tony knocked me down and sat on my neck for two hours.

Tony had been fighting on the ground for three years, he said. He'd gone to college to be a high-school social-studies teacher, but the job market was unforgiving and he'd adjusted his plan. He was now owner of a successful dog-walking business, not a bad way to spend your days, plenty of sunshine and fresh air.

"Everyone I work with is always happy to see me," he said. "How many people can say that?"

Tony talked about walking dogs while he pinned me and strangled me, until I tapped him to signal I'd had enough. Choke, tap, release, resume.

"Good grief," I said, coughing and snorting.

"Three years," he said.

My neck felt funny and I took a week off to recover. The next Tuesday morning, as I waited in the snow while he searched for his key to the front door, Cristiano said, "Where you been? You standing up today." He threw me in the cage with Brian, who dragged me by my arm into a side headlock. I slipped his hold as I started to see the twinkling lights, and I cranked his bent arm up behind his back in what my friend Russ used to call a chicken wing. The cops call that a hammerlock. The Brazilians call it a *kimura*. "Nice one, man," Brian said, surprised. Then he stomped on me for a little while.

✳

Ten years ago, after we'd been shooting nine-ball and drinking all day, my old friend Jay insisted on getting into a scuffle with half a defensive line in an empty lot outside the bar where my grandmother used to work at Third and Gaulbert. This was in Louisville.

"You're all right," one kid said to me, "but if your friend keeps asking for it, he's going to get it."

We'd already made it to my car, safe. Then Jay opened his door and charged at them. He got knocked flat, and the big boy he was tangling with crawled on top of him into what the Brazilians call the mount: sitting on Jay's chest with his knees up under Jay's armpits, Donkey Kong–ing on Jay's face while his confrères egged him on.

All right, I thought, what kind of friend am I, anyway, and I pushed my way into their circle and grabbed the kid on top of Jay by one of his shoulders.

"That's enough," I said.

"Tell him to say uncle," the kid said.

"Say uncle," I told Jay, and Jay said, "Uncle?"

"Are we straight now?" I said to the kid.

"Yeah. Okay," he said, and he got up and lumbered back into the bar.

"Open your mouth," I said to Jay. Two of his teeth were chipped. I put him back in the car and drove him to María's. I never did know what her story was. I think she loved him and she wanted to marry a U.S. citizen, both of those things.

"Oh God. What you do?" María said, while I stood there propping her boyfriend up on her porch, his bloody face print on my shoulder and chest. "Give him to me. I take care of him."

Jay called the next morning. "I don't know what happened, and I don't want to remember," he said. "Just tell me one thing. Do you look like me?"

I had to admit that I didn't. He hung up. I put the phone down and poured half a can of beer into half a glass of tomato juice as the back door opened.

"There's blood all over the inside of the Pontiac," my wife said.

And it was more or less in this manner that my wife became, as the years passed, my ex-wife. She moved to Nigeria and took an Islamic name, Djamila. It means *beautiful*.

✳

Brazilian jiu-jitsu comes in two flavors. There's the gi, that heavy cotton jacket you may have seen competitors wearing in judo, and there's no-gi, which is just what it sounds like. You use the gi's collar to choke your opponent, and you hold his pants or sleeves to control his movement. It's hard to escape from the grips and the friction. I wanted to learn about that, too, so I went to a Friday-night gi class.

I had expected my gi to be plain white, but it looked like a cross between subway graffiti and a full-page ad in *Cigar Aficionado*. On its back was a picture of a pit bull encircled by these words: *Gameness means that neither fatigue nor pain will cause the fighter to lose his enthusiasm for fighting contact.* I put it on and got to work. We did calisthenics and drilled chokes and armbars for an hour, then we sparred with one another.

At the end of the second hour, the head coach came by with a clipboard and a sign-up sheet. He had gray in his Afro and braces on his teeth.

"How long you practice?"

"This is my third day."

"You fight at tournament? End of February."

"If you think it's all right."

"Listen," he said. "After three days, is not like you try to kick nobody in ass or nothing. We go. Fight all day. Then big party. Okay?"

❋

I chose the gym because the fittest guy I knew—boxer, former NCAA gymnast, marathon runner—had gone to check it out and had gotten a couple of ribs broken for his trouble. That must be the real thing, I thought, that's the place for me.

It was on my fifth day of training that I realized how high the attrition rate was: many people do not like to get beaten up. I'd expected to be unremittingly dominated for at least six months, but there was a steady supply of beginners each weekend, and a mere eleven hours of experience was enough to provide a slight edge.

I rolled with a big kid and was surprised to find myself in control of the situation. "Come on, mate, get him. What did we just talk about?" his friend yelled from the sidelines.

"But he's a spider monkey," the kid said, gasping.

That was me: I was the spider monkey in question. I wrecked him. Then we changed partners and I got crushed by Noah and Courtney and Darryl—rear naked choke, armbar, arm triangle—as if I weren't even there. I went home and showered and searched for pictures of spider monkeys on the Internet.

✳

At or around this time I began to become *David*. I don't know why. It's my middle name, but that seemed to be a coincidence.

A lot of people turned around if you said *David*: David the software designer, Lebanese David, Speedy Dave the ex-boxer, Big David with his big smile and his shaved head, also the other big David with his own shaved head.

There were a lot of bald guys named David, and a preponderance of people named Big—Big Jim, Big John, Big Tony—not in order to differentiate them from, say, Minor Jim or Small Tony, it was just that they were so gigantic it was difficult not to mention it.

I wasn't big or bald. I was skinny and hairy. People said, "Hey, David," and I didn't look up—I didn't know who I was supposed to be, I didn't know who they were talking to.

I saw Cristiano again. "So you David now?" he said. "When this happen? Okay, David. Why you don't training in morning, David? Miss you in morning."

"I'm asleep."

"Sleep is bad habit, man."

"Just wait for the summer."

"Is summer now, already. Come see me in morning, David."

I had often wondered, filling out government forms that required me to disclose other names by which I might have been known, how a man acquired an alias. We began to get calls at the house from my new friends, wanting to train, looking for Dave.

"How long do you expect to be involved with this crap?" my girlfriend said.

"Go ask Jacob why he wrestled with the angel," I said. She rolled her eyes.

✳

At the tournament I fought no-gi, novice class, at 154 pounds. My opponent was five inches shorter than I was, thick and stone-jawed with a silver flat-top.

I scored a smashing single-leg takedown but dropped inside his closed guard and fell victim to his guillotine choke: he looped an arm around what one coach had called my giraffey neck and began to uproot my spine the way you pull a weed out of your garden. It was quick and painful, and I tapped out. I had been training for two months. The forearm I wiped under my nose came away slick with blood.

"You all right, David?" my coach said.

"I'm fine," I said. And it was true. I mean, I wasn't David, but I was all right.

Medic to mat four, medic to mat eleven: I had already seen a kid get choked unconscious. I had seen a guy pull on his foot to tighten a figure-four leg choke until he'd sprained his own ankle. I had seen a dislocated shoulder—maybe it wasn't technically dislocated, but I can promise you that is not where it's supposed to be located. I had seen a kid go out on a stretcher, his neck strapped to a board. I had seen a broken arm and some broken ribs and plenty of broken toes.

I shook my opponent's meaty hand. "Good luck," I said. "Now beat them all. I want to tell my friends I lost to the guy who won this whole division."

He blinked. "Hey, thanks, man," he said. Then he beat them all.

I decided not to fight in the next tournament.

*

I needed better wind. I had to stop smoking cigars. It's amazing, what you'll have to give up in this life. I used to think my uncle Charles was joking about waking up in a Dumpster in Tucson until I woke up in the bed of a pickup truck humming down I-64 in southern Illinois.

No more whiskey, no beer, no vodka, no gin, no wine, no brandy, no pot, no acid, no cocaine, no mushrooms, no opium, no nitrous, no Xanax, no Ritalin, no Thorazine—it's hard to believe that we ever took Thorazine *for fun*—no Vicodin, no Percodan, no Flexeril, no kidding.

I thought about not smoking while I sat on the pavement and smoked before my evening lecture. A bearded man in his late fifties, wearing a tattered safari vest and pushing a grocery cart down the street, turned and said, "Want a little booze? I don't mean no harm." He parked his cart and sat next to me. A pretty coed ran past us. "Slow down, girl," he called after her.

※

As I put on my tie and jacket one day after practice, Big Jim said, "Are you really a professor, Professor Dave? Did you have to go to school for, like, a long time?"

When Jim wasn't getting paid to beat people up in a cage, he had a part-time job delivering hot wings.

"Is being a teacher a good job? Do all the little schoolgirls sit on your lap?"

"I used to work down at the trailer plant with my dad," I said. "It's better than that."

"Where'd you find a place to go to school in Kentucky, anyway?" Dennis said. "I-eat-a-lot-of-fried-chicken University?"

"He went to KFCU," Steve said.

"Professor Dave went to F-U-C-K," Jim said.

"That's funny, man," Dennis said, not laughing.

※

At the next tournament I fought in gi and no-gi, and made it both times nearly to the end of my rounds before being *submitted*, as they say. I got triangled—caught in a figure-four choke that pressed on my carotid artery, cutting off the flow of blood to my brain and threatening me with unconsciousness—and I got knuckle-choked, a painful vise-grip in which the neck is crushed between the opponent's arm and opposite fist.

I sulked for two days and decided my main problem was general physical fitness. If you can't run, you're not fit. My knee hurt then and it hurts now. It's hurt for twenty years. I guess it's going to hurt for the rest of my life. Cambridge is lousy with runners, and every time one of those scarecrows breezed past me and my knee brace, I thought, I'm glad you can run, because when I catch you the ER nurse is going to pick your teeth out of my elbow the way Mamaw picked raisins out of her slice of cake. That impressed my knee for about four slow miles before the ligament I'd torn twenty years earlier turned back into garbage.

I went to the running-shoe store. "Can I help you find anything?" the kid at the counter said.

"I don't know," I said. "Where do you keep the shoes that when you buy them you actually go running in them? Because that's not the kind I bought last time."

He smiled. "I hate running so much," he said. "You have no idea."

※

And then one day my friend Jamie said, "Are you still doing your Brazilian thing? I'm giving a talk at a conference in Porto Alegre in September, and they comped me a double room."

Jamie is a biostatistician and an epidemiologist who writes papers with titles like *Adaptive Nonparametric Confidence Sets*: "Consider an observation $X(n)$ distributed according to a law $P(n)$ depending on a parameter θ," and so on. I don't understand it, and I don't need to understand it. What makes sense to me is a man who would rather do his work and eat a jar of mustard than interrupt himself with a trip to the grocery.

We touched down four minutes before Jamie's talk was due to start. He took a cab from the airport to his conference. I bought a ticket for another taxi, dropped our bags at the hotel, and headed to the gym. My driver looked around the neighborhood in question with some alarm.

Tudo bem, I said, and I got out of the cab and said *Boa tarde* to the nice young man who spent the rest of that week kicking me in my ear.

"Okay, now I angry dog. Where a snake looks? Look my eyes. His will in him eyes. Okay, I punch your face. Punching your face! No, no, okay, better, good. *Vai!* Loose hip. Don't previewing, take what he offering you. Okay. Slip and turn, hooks in. *Espalha frango*, break him down. Surf. How you don't surf?"

Off the mat, he was calm and kind, that young man. He gave me a lot of good advice.

"Fighting make my life," he said. "You know what you feel in fight. Excite, scare, now I kill him, oh God, don't hurt me, I win everything, I never win nothing, you know? And without fighting, when you feel this in your life? For someone else, is once in ten years, when he get marry, when son is born, when his father die. Two, three days in life, he feel this. Here you feel every day. Fear, happy, anger, strong, can I do it. No, I can't do it. Yes, I did it. It make you a more major person—is this right, *major*? It make him have his life."

He was ashamed to ask for money. "*Mas eu quero pagar*," I said. "*Eu vou pagar.*"

"Yes," he said. "I am not a mercenary, you understand. But we have to keep lights on. Why it is so expensive, you may wonder. You cannot teach to just anyone. Not, how do you say this, pit bully, fight unfair when he know he will win, stab you, hit you with a bat. Not this person. No. And this is why it is so expensive, it make him understand the value. I am sorry." Finally he asked me for fifty *reais*, about twenty dollars.

※

There were two things on television in Porto Alegre: pretty girls in bathing suits singing and

dancing, and solemn panels discussing José Sara-
mago and Joaquim Maria Machado de Assis. In the
display window of the average bookstore were
Sontag, Baudrillard, Borges, and Heidegger. I saw
men and women of astonishing beauty and self-
possession in that city, and I saw people as poor as
stray cats, not merely homeless but without clothing to wear, on Avenida Goethe and Rua Schiller.
I bought some Cohibas and a *cafezinho* and the
nice old man behind the counter wanted to know
what I was doing in his country. As little as possi-
ble, some tourism, some sports, do you like Brazilian jiu-jitsu, *senhor*? He put his hands up as if it
were a robbery and said in Portuguese, "Listen,
we're all friends here."

Every day after practice I had *feijoada* and col-
lard greens for lunch, and in the evenings, after
more practice, I went out with Jamie and his col-
leagues to fancy restaurants. One night a long blond
New Zealander in a short black dress asked me why,
if I wasn't an epidemiologist, was I sitting next to
her at a table of epidemiologists while taciturn gau-
chos fed us heaps of meat shaved from skewers. I
made my usual mistake of telling the truth.

"Really," she said. "And when I was a little girl
I wanted to be a Brazilian ballerina. Do you hear
this? He says he's doing something called *Brazilian
jiu-jitsu*. Go on, you're just ashamed to be an epide-

miologist, like all the rest of us. Now tell me another one," she said, moving closer and putting her
hand on my arm, but I didn't know another one. It
still wasn't altogether clear to me what epidemiol-
ogy was. An accordion wheezed. On a stage in the
center of the restaurant, men began to dance with
knives.

※

Back home in the States, I had a whanging bruise
in my ear. I had tendinitis in both wrists and a
sprained thumb. I had a broken toe, the first of many:
you just *buddy it up*, taping it to its intact neighbor,
and you go about your business. My neck sounded
like a marimba.

This hurts, that hurts, perhaps you should con-
sult your gynecologist. My girlfriend said, "I have
no pity for you. None. What happened to the book-
ish layabout I fell in love with?"

My friends at the gym weren't interested,
either, and I didn't plan to inform them. It was rare
to hear a fighter, especially a professional, admit to
pain.

"How was it last weekend?" I asked Jim.

"Great, man. I murdered him."

"No kidding?"

"Brutal. No chance. Stoppage at a minute fifty.
It was a slaughter."

"Is he okay?"

"I guess," Jim said. "I broke the bone of his nose with my elbow until it was sticking out of his face."

"Right on. How's your elbow?"

"It's fine, man. But you know what? My hand really stings."

He showed me a minuscule scratch on his knuckles. The lion, victorious, had earned the right to complain of a thorn in his paw.

✳

January 2009. A talented young man from our gym got signed to the *Ultimate Fighting Championship*, that mixed-martial-arts program you can see on your television, and he won his first fight. Later he won his second, then his third, then his fourth. Have you ever seen that show? It began to dawn on me how fortunate I had been to have survived for a year.

After an hour of circuit training, an hour of drills, and an hour of sparring, the owner of the gym came over and slapped me on my back. "Nice work, professor," he said. "Everyone else here today is a professional fighter." *Nice work*: I had a pair of bloody slashes from inadvertent elbows, one across my cheek, the other from my lower lip to my chin, God only knows what an intentional elbow might have done. I was ugly but I wasn't crippled, and it was in this way that I began to train more with the mixed-martial-arts pros.

"You don't look like such a hairy guy," one of them said, "but you take your shirt off and it's all *Teen Wolf.* I'm the same way if I don't shave it."

"You trying to tell me you shave your chest?"

"Got to shave that shit," he said, smiling. But I wasn't going to shave my chest.

What I liked best about the MMA guys was that they tended to forget we were at grappling practice. Somebody would get on top of me and get enthusiastic about his position of advantage and start punching me in the face, bare-knuckled. "Oh, hey, sorry, man," he'd say, coming to his senses after I'd eaten a couple of swats, and I'd say it's okay, forget about it, let's keep going. But almost nobody really likes getting hit in the face. After one practice I touched my nose and it made a little skutching sound.

"What is it now?" my doctor said.

"I want you to tell me if my nose is broken."

"It's broken," she said without looking up from her clipboard.

"But it's still straight."

"No, it isn't."

"But it doesn't hurt. I mean, it hurts, but not a lot."

"Uh-huh." She put her hand on my face. "How about this?"

"No."

"And this?"

"Gaah. Aaah."

"X-ray is down the hall," she said.

I filled half a dozen surgical gloves with tap water and froze them into V-shaped ice packs to balance on the bridge of my nose.

"You are mentally ill," my girlfriend said.

When Dennis saw the tape over my nose, he smiled and said, "What's that, a target?"

✳

Shoulder-stability push-ups on and off the medicine ball. High knees and sprawl drills. Honeymooners: "Shut up, pick up, stand up, run up. Now drop him and submit him," our coach said, "you know, just like your wedding night." Skip-step knees into the heavy bag. Farmer's walks. Dummy slams. Kettlebell swings. Medicine-ball Russian twists. Dead-hang knee raises. Mountain climbers. Planks and side planks. Into the weighted harness to run sled dogs, dragging the coach. Fireman's carries. Muay Thai clinch drills. V-sits, hitting the heavy bag, hitting the focus mitts, leg sparring with shin guards.

And there are also many other things, which, if they should be written every one, I suppose that even the world itself could not contain the books that should be written.

You learn a lot about yourself when you train to failure, when you go out to the edge of your ability, wherever that is.

"I can't finish, Mark," I said.

"Shut up, Dave. You can. Never can't."

"I have to throw up."

"Go ahead."

"I have to shit."

"No, you don't."

"I'm going to shit."

"Not during my drill, you aren't. Finish my drill."

I finished and staggered to the bathroom, where only I was surprised to find that I had no urge whatsoever. "And these last ten, they better than first ones," our coach yelled at me. "Can you make me to understand this, David? How you try to show I can't do no more, then five more best, then ten more better? Don't stop, go. And don't be mad at me right now. Okay, David and Andre. Andre, kill him, please. Joey, you come here. Oh my God, Joey, you just twenty years old. How you going to be when you thirty, man, you dead already."

※

I was becoming hard to live with. One night in bed my girlfriend said, "Honey, don't do any of that jiu-jitsu crap to me." It's tough to spend much time rolling around on the floor with a bunch of sweaty guys without admitting that sex and violence are drawn from the same well. Remember what you told that kid on the playground: *I'm going to fuck you up.*

I kept getting skin infections. Ringworm (*tinea corporis*) sounds revolting, but it was an easy home cure with topical ketoconazole. Flat warts (*verruca plana*, a human-papillomavirus subtype) had to be removed with liquid-nitrogen-induced surgical frostbite. That hurt, and was expensive, and left nasty purple-and-brown scars on my forearms.

I was smelly and tired. "Get me some paper towels, will you?" my girlfriend said. I went into the closet and came back with a gallon of water. "Paper towels, honey." I put the water away and came back with a different gallon. "Honey, I need those paper towels." I put that gallon away and returned with a roll of paper towels and a third gallon of water. "Now can you open them for me?" I opened the water and took a drink.

✳

I couldn't pay attention to anything without some relation, however tangential, to Brazil. I read Skidmore's *Brazil: Five Centuries of Change* and Eakin's *Brazil: The Once and Future Country*. I read Levine's *The History of Brazil* and Burns's *A History of Brazil* and MacLachlan's *A History of Modern Brazil*. I read Rubem Fonseca's *High Art* and Caio Fernando Abreu's *Whatever Happened to Dulce Veiga?* and Patrícia Melo's *The Killer* and began to recognize a subgenre of Brazilian literature: the noir novel where people smoke cigarettes, talk about Roland Barthes, and now and then stick the handle of a hunting knife up somebody's behind. I ripped through Ignácio de Loyola Brandão's jagged *Zero*. I endured Antônio Callado's pious *Quarup*. I read most of Ivan Ângelo's *The Celebration*. I couldn't finish João Guimarães Rosa's *The Devil to Pay in the Backlands* although it was good—God knows I tried. I reread Machado de Assis, author of *Quincas Borba: Philosopher or Dog?* and *Dom Casmurro* and *The Posthumous Memoirs of Bras Cubas*. I read Appleby's biography of Heitor Villa-Lobos. I read the poetry of Carlos Drummond de Andrade. I read Peter Robb's *A Death in Brazil* and Peter Fleming's wonderful *Brazilian Adventure*.

Yo soy aficionado a leer, aunque sean los papeles rotos de las calles—I am very fond of reading, writes Cervantes, even torn papers in the streets.

For many years I had loved João Ubaldo Ribeiro's brilliant *Sergeant Getúlio*, a novel so good it shouldn't be buried in a long list. I read it again.

※

And I read Clarice Lispector. Here's a thing that happens sometimes. Karen says, "But don't you like any female writers?" and you say, "I don't keep score," and she says, "Let's give it a try." "Natalia Ginzburg is a good writer," you say, and she says, "Natalia Ginzburg is a man." You say, "I like Dubravka Ugrešić," and she says, "Man." You say, "I guess Flannery O'Connor is a man, too," and she groans and looks out the window. Doris Lessing, Marguerite Yourcenar, Jean Rhys, Patricia Highsmith, Joan Didion, Iris Murdoch—until you say, "Listen, if all women are men, then no, I can't think of any female writers I like."

And now it's time to have an argument. That's a thing that happens, sometimes.

You say, "What about Clarice Lispector?" and she says, "Who's Clarice Lispector?"

＊

I'd wanted to be a writer for a long time, almost thirty years. A writer, what a dream. I spent my twenty-seventh summer in Kentucky working as a night watchman doing twelve-hour shifts, eating fried mushrooms from the Moby Dick across the street before it closed at 8:00 p.m., nine hours to go, downing pseudoephedrine bronchodilators to stay awake, drinking King Cobra to manage the consequent anxiety, smoking Macanudos and banging away on my portable typewriter in the back room of the flower-and-fruit market I was protecting from no one but an occasional stray dog until the bar across the street disgorged its staggering belligerents at three the next morning, and they weren't much of a threat: I told them to fuck off, and they fucked off. All I did was sleep and tell people to fuck off, perhaps identifying my vocation, and I saved a lot of money that summer.

Then I moved to Boston and met some professional writers, and developed a more realistic idea of what I'd gotten myself into. I had always assumed that a writer had adventures and met other people, and then told a story about what had happened, or else just made the whole thing up, or both. Now it looked like what a professional writer did was *pontificate*, you know, like the Pope, about social justice and foreign affairs and the Internet and the energy crisis. But I had formed myself on the Ruskin model. "The greatest thing a human soul ever does in this world is to *see* something and tell what it *saw* in a plain way": thus John Ruskin, who was terrified of pubic hair.

Above all, a professional writer had the correct opinions, and I couldn't figure out what they were. I was asked to write something for *The New Republic*, and I sent my copy and never heard from them again. I was asked to write something for the

London Review of Books, and that was bought but it never ran. I was asked to write something for *GQ*, but I couldn't make that happen, either.

I was ruining big chances left and right, and it was nobody's fault but mine, and I was twenty-eight years old, twenty-nine, thirty, thirty-one, and soon all I wanted to do was beat the shit out of somebody.

I wanted to beat the shit out of somebody, or else I wanted the shit beaten out of me, apparently either one was fine, and a good thing too, because it turned out there was plenty of that to go around: the beating of shit out of me, is what I mean.

Fighting was an adequate substitute for writing. I got in a couple of fights, under controlled circumstances, almost every day, sometimes before breakfast. A fight is a story. It offers the shaped comfort of narrative: a beginning, *first this happened*, and a middle, *then this happened because of that*—and, if it is not interrupted, an end.

※

June 2009. As the third tournament approached, I realized I was going to have to cut some pounds to make my weight class. I had been on the "seafood diet": whenever you see food, you eat it.

"Honey, I can't stand this," my girlfriend said. "You're so irritable when you're hungry. I'm going to stay in New York until it's over." She went south and I went feral. I skipped meals and I skipped rope, and at last I sweated my way back to 155, where I wanted to be. I drove to Rhode Island for the pre-fight weigh-ins, after which I drank two Gatorades and half a gallon of water and peed right there in the parking lot next to my car like the drunken id-iot I had once been: *drunken* no more, fossilized *idiot* part remarkably intact. Next, standing there in the smell of my own urine, I ate a cold sausage pizza, then two bananas, then a bagful of roasted almonds. On the way back, I ate half a loaf of bread and drank the other half of the gallon of water. At home, I ate a big steak salad and the other half of the loaf of bread and some chocolate cake and ice cream. And the next morning I weighed 163 pounds.

These were the rules as announced over the loudspeaker:

> All submission techniques are legal, includ-ing heel hooks, knee locks, neck cranks, guillotine chokes, et cetera . . . No elbows or forearm strikes, no butting with the head, no knees to the head, no hand strikes, no kicks. No attacks to the front of the wind-pipe, eyes, or groin. No pushing palm or elbow directly into nose. No dropping or slamming of opponent on head . . . Eye

gouging, fishhooking, biting, pulling hair,
pinching, twisting of skin, sticking a finger
into a cut of an opponent, . . . and putting a
finger into any orifice—

"Does that include the butthole?" Big Will said.

—are all fouls and grounds for disqualifi-
cation . . . Please wear clean clothing.

I shook my opponent's hand and dragged him to
the mat into my closed guard, controlling his pos-
ture, and we got to work. I whipped one of my legs
over his arm and trapped his neck and other arm
in a figure-four, a too-loose triangle choke. As he
struggled to stand up, I hooked his leg and swept
him, rolling him over. Then, sitting on his chest,
I let go of the triangle and hooked my outside leg
over his face while I kept his arm, pinching it between my knees, and I leaned back and shoved my
hips into his elbow, bending it the way it doesn't go.
That did the trick. He tapped. The ref stopped the
fight. I let my opponent up and hugged him. I was
so happy. Someone handed me a medal. I wore it.

Later that same day, I caught a pair of losses in
my gi division, one of them astonishing in its speed.
"Who cares?" Dennis said. "Look around you. Who's
here? You see all those people who aren't here? Do

you know why you don't see them? It's because *they aren't here*. But you are here. You showed up and did your work. Try to relax, man. You can't win them all." It was news to me that I could win any of them.

※

What next? What else: I made a sickening cut to 148 to fight as a featherweight, so weak and hungry that my hair hurt, and I came in third at yet another tournament. My face looked like a sandwich someone had already eaten: everything, really, looked like food to me. I had night sweats and a nasty cough.

"I don't like the sound of this," my doctor said, frowning at her stethoscope, and it turned out I did have to stop smoking in the end, if this is *the end*. There's no *at last*, it's not *the end*, there is no curtain, it does not fall.

I took eight weeks off to squat and dead-lift heavy and eat everything that wasn't nailed down, and I gained thirty-five pounds and had to buy new pants. Then I went back to sparring and I broke a guy's ribs. That was nice.

And then I did it all again, the way you find yourself eating dinner again the next night; the way you have sex, if you do, again; the way too much to drink was barely enough. It didn't end, it doesn't end, and if I knew what to say next, this wouldn't be the end.

※

The angel said to Jacob, Let me go, for the day breaketh; and Jacob said, I will not let thee go except thou bless me. That was all he wanted.

So the angel said, What is thy name? Thy name shall be called no more Jacob, and the angel blessed him. And Jacob let the angel go.

LETTER FROM MAJORCA

Let's suppose you are a serious person, or you transmit to yourself certain conventional signals of a sort of seriousness: you reread Tacitus, you attempt to reread Proust but it can't be done, you listen to Bartók and to Archie Shepp.

Also: You can't stop moving your bowels, or your body can't. You have a body, you are a body. You don't know what's safe to eat these days, or when. You're so sick that you take off your clothes when you use the bathroom, for safety's sake. That was a hard lesson to learn.

Let's stop saying *you*.

I had a body. It was a problem. It hurt most of the time. I dreamt of one world and woke into another. My throat hurt, my stomach hurt, I coughed, I lay in bed and stared at the ceiling and thought about death. I heard its soft footfalls approaching. I had some blood tests, I took some medicine. I spent a lot of time in bed.

At the time I'm telling you about, I was earning some money, not much, as a freelance journalist and a teacher in a university, writing about education, about gun control, about fashion or music, reviewing new novels through a haze of rage and envy, telling myself that *whatever it takes* means *whatever it takes*, doing whatever I had to do to convince myself that I was not a number-two schmuck.

The wife tells her husband: You must be the number-two schmuck in the whole world.

Why can't I be the number-one schmuck? he says.

But how could you be number one? she says. You're such a schmuck.

There was nothing the matter with me that was not also the matter with everyone else. I was not as interesting as I thought I was. My major problem, inadequate or inappropriate love from my parents, was as common as dirt.

And one rainy day, all the boring poignancy of these realizations detonated in me like an atom bomb, burning the dead shadow of each former torment or preoccupation onto solid rock. Those silhouettes, that record would remain: the museum where I used to be.

All right, I thought, I've had enough. Some other way from now on, but not like that, not anymore.

✳

And so I quit the university after shouting at a student until she began to cry. "You're crying?" I said. "Why are you crying?" She ran away.

I had done this to innumerable boys over the years and had considered it good for them, but a girl's tears shocked me and made me see myself as I was: cruel, power-mad, an abuser of children, because in our time twenty-year-olds remain children, and they themselves are not entirely to blame. We have failed them. Let's stop saying *we*.

I shouted at a pretty girl with long black hair. She often stayed after class to discuss her favorite books with me, sitting next to me on my desk, playing with the strap of her tank top and smiling in a way that becomes familiar to every teacher, flattering and dangerous, and when she ran away crying I saw that I had scolded her in order to prevent myself from going to bed with her.

And later, when I realized that her name, she had a man's first name, was also the name of a friend with whom I was angry because I had praised my analyst in his presence and he had applied and been taken on as an analysand, when I realized that by driving my student away I was also murdering her name-twin, my rival sibling, I thought: These kids deserve better instruction than I am currently capable of providing.

Once I admitted how much I wanted to kill and eat the children who had been entrusted to my care,

I tried to forgive myself for any harm I might have done them over the years, for all the crackling bolts I had hurled from my cloud of self-serving ignorance, and I left that institution of learning to resume my position of nothingness in a world where I had no power to abuse my subordinates because I had no subordinates, where I had no authority save whatever I might seize by force or by cunning—where, as each day proves afresh, people will walk smiling through puddles of your blood, smiling and talking on their cellular phones. They're going to the movies.

※

People at parties in Cambridge asked me *What do you do?* with alarming regularity. I had spent the previous thirty years in Kentucky never once having been asked what I did, because what would be the point: I do some task I don't care about in order to be able to afford to stay alive, the same as you do, and then I clock in at my real job, holding down a stool at the Back Door or Check's Cafe or Freddie's Bar-Lounge or Jake's Club Reno.

In Cambridge, at parties, I said whatever came first into my mind.

"I manufacture organic catheters."

"I'm a butt scientist."

"I am an AM/FM clock radio."

For a while, when I sensed they might find it contemptible, I threw into people's faces that I worked in a deli. It was true: once, in Cambridge, I made a sandwich for Arthur M. Schlesinger, Jr. "I think that was Arthur Schlesinger," I said, and the next person in line said, "Who's Arthur Schlesinger?"

And once I made a Reuben for a Weimaraner. Probably I made a lot of sandwiches for dogs without knowing it, but the lady I am thinking of made it clear to me that I was to be careful with her dog's sandwich: "Take it easy on the Russian dressing."

I was proud of myself on the day I quit my university teaching job. I remembered when I was still a little boy and my father came home from work, too tired and sore to bend over and take his own boots off, and I was so pleased to take his boots off for him, the brown-and-white laces and the brads and the dry mud flaking onto the floor, and my mother said, "How was work today?" and my father said, "I quit."

We sat down to dinner and we did not speak. Soon the phone rang, and my father smiled. On the phone was someone who had heard about how my father had told the foreman off, good, he deserved it and only you had the guts to give it to him, we always have a job for a man like you, can you start tomorrow. He could.

Now that it was settled, we finished eating our

dinner, meatloaf and mashed potatoes maybe, or hamburgers and thick-cut deep-fried potatoes, my father's favorite. And that night my mother sobbed until she vomited. This happened many times when I was a boy.

I told my girlfriend I had quit my job. "That was dumb," she said.

❋

It was at this time that the captain called me long-distance from Tunisia and said, "I need a man. Get over here."

"I'm sick," I said. "I don't know how much help I can be to you."

"All I need is arms and legs," he said. "Do you still have arms and legs? Then buy a ticket for Cagliari and meet us in Carloforte."

The captain was a gray giant out of Tel Aviv. One holiday I had seen him surrounded by his daughters, by his sons-in-law, his grandchildren, his pretty young girlfriend, and I had thought: This man has something to teach you about what a certain kind of happiness is in life, so learn it, you dummy.

I already felt *at sea* as they say, *lost in familiar places* is another thing they say. I decided to spend some time at sea, where my bewilderment might make more sense, because disorientation and chaos would actually be happening.

Why do people feel things and go places, tell me if you know.

❋

That was how my odyssey began. I flew to Heathrow Terminal 4, where a man in one of the many airport bars drank a bottle of Worcestershire sauce, put the empty in his briefcase, and chased it with a pint of ale. A morose Russian paced near Aeroflot. I flew on to Sardinia and hired a car, and soon I was alone, under the moon, without the luggage Alitalia had lost, on the last ferry to the island called San Pietro.

The boat was forty-three feet long and there were five of us, myself and four Israelis, on it for five weeks. I had never been sailing for more than two hours at a time, in Boston Harbor. I didn't understand the captain when he told me to take the French seasickness pill.

There was work to be done and so after three acid-yellow heavings-up they left me to my fate, sprawled on my back with a bucket nearby. Shattered by nausea and fear, I sweated through my shirt and took it off and wrung it out and wiped myself with it. I was sick all day and night as we crossed from Sardinia to Minorca. I hadn't had a drink in eight years but hello, vomiting, it is always nice to see you again.

When the captain saw that I could sit up and drink water, he said, "You're a sailor now," and he sent me fore. It wasn't true that I was a sailor but it was true that a task helped me to focus on something other than my constant boring suffering, something to do with the jib roller, it's all a blur.

I wasn't going to be sick again for more than a month, but there was no way I could know that. As we hobbyhorsed up and down, pitching hard over the waves, I saw first the sea and then the sky, black sea, night sky, burning moon, a foretaste of death.

Both Odysseus and Captain Ahab are heroes of departure and return, for Ahab, too, returns: to his death-home, in the whale.

※

Shlomo's English was good. He told me about the Dead Sea Scrolls. He told me about Brazilian agronomy. He told me about Joseph Stiglitz.

Shlomo said, "I ask myself, who are the wisest people in the world? The answer is the Jews. This is well-known.

"And who are the wisest Jews? A moment's reflection reveals that Russian Jews are the wisest.

"Next we must discover who are the wisest of these Russian Jews. And the answer comes back, clearly the people of Odessa.

"So who are the wisest Jews in Odessa? The members of the old synagogue.

"It's plain to see, then, that the wisest man in the world must be Rabbi Loew, chief rabbi of the old synagogue of Odessa. But he's such an idiot."

*

And Amatsia said, "My brain is fucking."

He meant his memory was going bad. Asked for an example, he explained that in the army he had once carried a dead man on his back for two days and now he couldn't remember the man's name.

He shook his head. "Fucking," he said.

Amatsia didn't talk much. He smoked. Every now and then he picked up the binoculars and looked at the colors of the flags of other ships and said, "Fucking Germans."

One night, docked, we met a German couple in a Spanish restaurant. "You talk about Jerusalem, I think," the man said, "in your beautiful language. It is so interesting. I, too, have been to *Yerushalayim*, so interesting. Yes, and to Haifa, also. A beautiful city."

The captain said, "Do you know what we say about the beautiful Haifa?"

"What is that?"

"The most beautiful thing in Haifa is the road to Tel Aviv."

All the Israelis, a little drunk, laughed.

"Yes," the German said, "this is a kind of humor, I think."

※

Amatsia had sailed across the Atlantic Ocean with the captain ten years earlier. He smoked, and I smoked, too, pretending to be him, because I wanted to fit in and because he seemed to be an admirable man, quiet and hardworking, and from time to time the captain snarled at us in Hebrew.

"He says smoking is stupid," Amatsia said.

I smoked a cigar on a bench along the dock and saw a waterfront bum coming from a hundred yards away. He was burned brown and wrinkled by the sun. He looked like a wallet someone had been sitting on for forty years.

"Have you got another *puro*?" he said. "You speak English? You understand me? Don't worry about Spanish. English is the best. A very good language. With English, you go anywhere in the world. All places. If you know Spanish, what does that get you? Tell me, where can you go?" He made a face as he gestured around himself, disgusted by the beauty of his native Spain.

※

It had been a long time since Señorita Geile had taught me Spanish with her hand puppet named

Teodoro, a little bear. I had written the Pledge of Allegiance, *juro fidelidad a la bandera de los Estados Unidos de América*, as a punishment when I was bad, which had been often, and I had memorized *poesía*, but now I couldn't remember one word of it, which is not what *memorize* means. I memorized the Pledge of Allegiance, and I memorized this fact: I am bad.

A cab driver said to me, "How many languages do you speak? Your Spanish is very bad, we're not going to count that one." He adjusted his eyeglasses and said, "The real money in this cab-driving business is the night shift, the *putas*. Tell me something. How do you say *fucky-fucky* in English?"

I floated in a sea of Hebrew, or in an estuary of Spanish and Hebrew. I made up ways to spell what I thought I was hearing. It's astonishing what you won't need to know in this life. I got by for weeks with nothing but *ani rotse le'echol mashehu bevakasha*, which means, I think, *I want something to eat, please.*

I thought about language—speaking in tongues, rebuking the Devil—and I thought about twins: about my new sibling, the fellow analysand I loved and had shared my precious analyst with and now wanted to kill. I would kill him and eat him. Maybe I would eat him first.

There were twins at my high school, nice shy Vietnamese boys. They were king-hell math achievers but they hardly spoke a lick of English. At first I figured they spoke French at home, or Vietnamese, but I came to understand that they didn't speak those languages, either. They'd had each other since birth, before language, and they had never seen the need to learn to speak anything.

※

The Israelis were competitive in all things, and they soon set out to establish who was the greatest shipboard cook. The contest lasted for weeks and was delicious, but I was often sick, and there was the small problem of the head on board. I made it filthy, sometimes twice, because I was sick, and then I made it clean again, not without some effort. I have cleaned a lot of toilets, I worked as a janitor at one time, and I can tell you land-based toilets are preferable, they do not move.

Shlomo wouldn't take his turn cleaning the head. "It stinks," he said.

"The head smells fine," said the captain. "What stinks is human shit."

We could urinate over the side if the sea wasn't too rough. "One hand for you, one hand on the ship," the captain said, "and no matter what lies she may have told you, boys, one hand for yourself is plenty. Most of the dead men in the sea have their flies open."

＊

On the boat, we did laundry like this. You wore your underwear until you felt you were no longer a member of the human race. Then you turned it inside out and wore it some more.

I found myself thinking about my father, about a time we had gone to a baseball game together. We were in the parking lot.

"When are you moving north?" he said.

"The forty-third of Delfember," I said, and he laughed, and then he said, "Help me," and I turned around and my father had shit in his britches.

He'd been out the night before with his best friend, Jeff, a bartender who was blind in one eye and drunk in the other and tended to wear a black T-shirt that said VIETNAM VETERAN, in case any onlookers happened to wonder if Jeff might be a veteran and, if so, of what conflict.

And when I say *tended* I mean he wore that shirt to funerals, a T-shirt at a funeral, that was Jeff all the way. When his own brother, when Jeff's brother, Sarge, died, my father lent him my mother's car and Jeff, already crocked at ten in the morning, almost ran it off the road on his way to the service, scraping it along the guardrail and snapping off its side mirror. My mother said nothing, which was not her habit.

My father, too, was a Vietnam veteran. So were a lot of men in my family. One of them was my uncle, who died of Agent Orange–related complications.

"Let that be a lesson to you," my father said. "Don't join the service, and don't let your friends join the service. Because they tell you what to do. They tell you where to go, they tell you what to eat. They tell you when to die. And then you're dead."

※

In that parking lot, my father was right to trust in my expertise. I was well acquainted with the problem at hand. I was a promising young drunk, bad with women and an easy vomiter, and occasionally I had to shit as well. I had shit the bed once and kept sleeping and got up in the morning, going happily about my day off, and had not noticed until my then wife came home from her job and asked me what it might be in our bedroom that smelled so much like shit. And, of course, it was shit that smelled that way. That was the answer.

And so I was prepared to aid my father. As in so many endeavors, the first step is to lie: I said everything was going to be just fine. I told him he had to be brave for a few minutes, could he do that, could he walk, if not we could find some other way but that would be the simplest, and he said he thought he could. We walked past the parked cars and trucks and the yellow paint on the asphalt toward the gray concrete of the arena and its public restroom. I got my father into a stall and stood outside and told him to take his shoes and socks and jeans and underwear off.

My father hated public restrooms. Once, when I was a little boy, I had noticed he did not wash his hands after urinating and asked him about that habit and he had given his explanation, saying, "I'm confident that my penis is the cleanest thing in this environment."

His drawers were not so bad after all, but I threw them in the garbage just to seem like I was doing something to help. I passed him handfuls of paper towels.

"Check your legs down to your ankles and feet," I said. "Check your socks. How are your pants? We want to keep them."

"What if we can't?"

"Then you wear my shirt around your waist like a kilt until we get back to the truck," I said.

But he washed and dried himself and put his pants and socks and shoes back on. And that was that. It was nothing he could not have done on his own if he had given it a moment's thought.

Orders make you stupid, the captain told me, *figure it out for yourself.*

※

What do you know, I'm finally shitting my father. God knows I ate enough of him. I am thirty-seven years old, five feet ten inches tall, 180 pounds, a hairy man like Esau with an increasing amount of gray in my chest, a miniature facsimile of my father is half-extruded from my rectum, otherwise I am in good health.

The past is behind me, burning, like a hemorrhoid. My parents will not die if I wish them dead. They will die because life is finite.

When I was in college, one of my teachers said, "What's the matter with you? Are you waiting for your parents to die before you write anything honest?" and I said, "That is the dumbest question I have ever heard."

✳

My mother calls collect from hell. She rides her bike and goes swimming. There are a lot of ibises in hell. She sends me a picture. It's pretty.

I'm shouting into the telephone, I'm trying to shout but it's hard to make a noise, my jaw won't work, my teeth are long and getting longer, they break against each other, everywhere I turn I'm biting something. I bite the telephone, biting.

My parents are not dead. I mean hell on earth, plain old regular *real* hell. You know that hell? That's the one I'm talking about. And even when they are dead they will live on in me, burning in my hell-head, it's so crowded in here, still yammering about what I ought to do. Now I see how it is, you drop a coat hanger on the floor and if no one is watching you don't pick it up, that's the kind of man you've become. My dead father in particular is very interested in the proper configuration of everyday household items like coat hangers.

＊

Ibiza was on fire as we approached by night from the sea. A third of the island was burning. We anchored and watched airplanes swoop to fill their tanks with seawater. They flew high over the mountains and dropped water on the burning trees again and again. It was the biggest wildfire on the island in all of recorded history. It was still burning the next day when we left.

Shlomo, swimming just before we pulled up anchor, was stung by a jellyfish. "Do you want me to pee on it?" I said.

"No, I want you to shit on it," he said. "Americans!" he said.

＊

On that boat, surrounded by blank water and blank Hebrew, with a somewhat less blank Spanish awaiting me on shore, I was free from the obligation to apprehend and interpret. If I don't understand what you want from me, I don't have to try to do it, I can't.

The sea is incomprehensible and uncomprehending, the sea doesn't care, which is terrific, depending on what kind of *care* you are accustomed to receiving. The sea is wet.

As a teenager I was once waved through a roadblock by a police officer who then pulled me over and ticketed me for running the roadblock. "I don't understand what you want from me," I said, something I had already, at that early age, said many times to many different people.

"What's the matter with you?" the officer snarled, something many different people have said to me, and when my father and I went to court we found I had been charged with attempting to elude a police officer and failure to comply. My father knew the judge, or should I say the judge knew my father: she had been his girlfriend in high school. My father and I were wearing the nicest clothes we owned.

"Well, Mr. Prosecutor, what do we have here?" the judge said, smiling.

"The apple doesn't fall far from the tree," said Mr. Prosecutor, and he was also smiling, and they were speaking to and for my father, not to me, although I had been charged with *attempting to elude a police officer*, for Christ's sake, I still don't understand it. I got off with a fine for making an illegal turn. The judge knew my father, everyone knew my father, just as everyone had known my grandfather, and even people who had not been alive at the time knew that all the lights in Hodgenville, Kentucky, had gone out when my grandfather died.

I was not a tree, I was an apple, I had not fallen far from those trees but I had fallen. Somewhere there had been an apple and a fall. This much we knew.

✳

If anyone wanted something from me on that boat, he said my name. If no one said my name, I was not wanted. And *I was not wanted*, I floated for a month in a sea of unmeaning noise, I was free from the horror of being deformed by another person's needs and desires.

I became a twin, a sibling to myself, and I gnawed myself for nourishment in the red cavern of the womb, relaxing into my own death.

I ate myself until there was nothing left but my mouth. Then I ate my own mouth. Then I died.

✳

But no one ever dies. I got off the boat and hailed a cab and took a train to Madrid.

In Madrid I went to the Prado, where I looked at Goya's *Saturno devorando a su hijo*. There he sat, sickened, with his horrid mouthful, and the whites of his eyes were huge.

I had always thought of Saturn as vicious, as power-mad. I had never realized how frightened he was, compelled to commit and experience horror against his will. I began to cry. I felt sorry for Saturn. He didn't want to eat anyone. His stomach hurt. He wasn't even hungry.

And I flew home. Last night I dreamt the Devil bit my penis off. This morning it was still there, or *here*. Where I am is called *here*.

LETTER FROM KENTUCKY

John C. Skaggs was born in Green County in 1805, thirteen years after Kentucky became our fifteenth state. His son, Ben Skaggs, was born in 1835 in Bald Hollow and married Missouri Ann Carter.

Their second-eldest boy, Will Franklin Skaggs, had his pick of Pleasant Poteet's granddaughters. He could have had Delilah or Myrtie Scripture, but he chose Ella Green Poteet. Their third child, after Carter C. and Elvie Omen, was Sylvia May.

Meanwhile, in Larue County, Elmina G. Dixon married Bryant Young Miller's boy, and they bore a girl they called Mary Bothena Doctor Bohanan Sarah Lucritia Miller Rock, who, mercifully, named her own son Charlie.

And Thomas Jefferson Quinley's daughter Sefronia married Edwin Russell Wheatley, and begat Mildred Lucille, who married Robert Raymond Salisbury, who called himself Butch Daniels—of whom we will not speak.

Their son married Charlie and Sylvia's daughter, and begat me: "His Majesty the Ego," as Freud wrote in 1908, "the hero of all daydreams and all novels."

This happened in Kentucky, except for the Freud part. That happened in Austria.

✳

I was born in Kentucky and lived there for the better part of three decades.

As schoolchildren we were taught that the word *Kaintuckee* came from *Ka-ten-ta-teh*, which meant, in Cherokee, "the dark and bloody ground."

Later they said *Ken-tah-ten* meant "future land" in Iroquois. In high school, they claimed it was Wyandot for "land of tomorrow," and I recall a field trip to see a documentary with that name.

Before long, historians were telling us it could be Seneca for "place of meadows," or it might be a Mohawk word, *Kentah-ke*, meaning "meadow."

And from time to time there was an expert, often but not always on a barstool, who argued that the region in its pristine state had seemed to its settlers to be nothing but wild turkeys and river canebrakes: *Kaneturkee*.

It was clear that no one had any idea what he was talking about—and, in this manner, the most valuable part of our education was received.

✳

I flew back to Kentucky on a cold spring day aboard a paper airplane that every sneeze of wind knocked sideways. Next time I'll swim. Everyone hates flying. Even birds hate flying.

A sign in the airport said LOUISVILLE WELCOMES TOGETHER FOR THE GOSPEL NAZARENE YOUTH INTERNATIONAL 2012 PENTECOSTAL FIRE YOUTH CONFERENCE. There was nowhere to sleep. The many hotel rooms of downtown Louisville were occupied by boys and men in red T-shirts with white crucifixes ironed on. They stood in traffic, gawking.

Someone had cut down the peach tree in the front yard of my old Preston Street house. There was a scrap of vinyl siding across the front step, and plastic wrap on the inside windows to keep out the draft, and wax paper fluttering under a gap in the door.

Across the street from that house had once been the only bar where they had known what I wanted, a shot of Jim Beam and a suitcase bottle of Sterling, and Bill set it up every time he saw me coming. It was called B & B Bar, said to have been named for its owner, Bill, and then for Bill again, because what kind of name is the B-Bar.

I had seen an old man get shot in front of that

bar because he wouldn't give two kids his bicycle. I snorted pills off the back of the toilet in that bar with a woman I didn't understand was a prostitute: but later it became clear to me.

Blind John, still dripping rain from his trip to the ATM, offered me a hundred dollars to let him go down on me.

"I think you're in the wrong bar," I said.

"Maybe you are," he said.

I lost a lot of money shooting nine-ball in that bar. Listen to your uncle Tim-Tom and never play pool for money against a man called Doc.

I saw a little man stab a big man with a carving knife on that bar's front steps. Later the wet knife glimmered under the streetlight on the hood of a prowl car. The big man went to the hospital. The little man went to the penitentiary. I don't know where the bar went.

※

I drove down to the tractor-trailer plant where my father had managed the repair shop, but the plant had closed. I had worked there twice.

The first time was in the touch-up shop with Orville, soldering brake-light wires and repainting trailers Andrew had banged his forklift into, as a summer job and as a warning from my father. This was the kind of job I was going to wind up with if

I didn't straighten up and fly right. I was the only man in that garage with ten fingers.

The second time was in the decal shop as a college dropout. I had not straightened up, I had not flown right, this was the kind of job I had wound up with.

By day, Mayflower trailers, Frito-Lay trailers, Budweiser and Bud Light trailers, Allied trailers. By night, drinking Colt 45 with Allen down by the train trestles, and later Boyd crawling around on the floor with a cardboard box on his head, insisting that he was a Christmas present.

I read *The Faerie Queene*—counting syllables, thinking about the number seven—and thought: One of these days I am going to jump off the Second Street Bridge.

*

Finley's was gone, too, nothing but a pile of bricks. At Indi's, eating the rib tips with red sauce and macaroni and cheese and mashed potatoes and gravy, I listened: "You never know. That's what I told them at his funeral this morning. I said, *all right, see you later.* But I was wrong."

And I remembered my friend Allen asking me if I saw a plain white van parked across from his house down by the racetrack.

Allen said, "Tell me something, man. The van

is real? I'm not paranoid? It's been parked there for days. Three days."

"I am sure that is true."

"Listen—am I crazy? Could it be the FBI?"

"Allen," I said, seated in his forest of pot plants, "let me ask you a question. What amount of drugs and paraphernalia is in your house, do you think? And what is it the FBI gets paid to do all day? I am one hundred percent certain it is the FBI. I will see you later."

I said, *see you later*; but I was wrong. I did not see Allen later. Allen went to jail.

✳

I took the Gene Snyder Freeway out to the Bible College and got off at Beulah Church and drove past AMF Derby Lanes ("all you can bowl") and Highview Church of God and Highview Baptist Church and Victory Baptist Church Camp.

An old woman with a long gray ponytail was doing yard work, cutting back bushes I had planted in front of the house where I had grown up, where I had tried to grow up. A tired black dog lay in the yard, her yard now, not mine.

It's an old story. The horse knows the way to carry the sleigh: you go back to the place, but the place isn't there anymore.

I drove out of Fern Creek down Bardstown

Road toward Buechel, past Cash Xpress and Mister Money, past Xtreme Auto Sounds and Ventura's Used Tires and Global Auto Glass, and past the Heart of Fire City Church, the pastor of which had once helped us move some furniture and when it came time for my mother to write him a check for his services he said, "Don't cheat a blind man, sister, I can't read."

I drove to my uncle Charles's house out in Okolona, past Latino Auto Service and The Godfather (the strip joint that once had on its marquee THE MAYOR IS GAY PLEASE SUE SO I CAN PROVE IT), past Liquor Palace 5 and Discount Medical Supplies, past Furniture Liquidators Home Center, past Cash America Pawn and Cashland, past The Mower Shop, past Los Mezcales and El Molcajete, past Big Ron's Bingo and Cashtyme Cash Advance ("You're Good For It!"), past Moore's Sewing & Learning Center, and DePrez's Quality Jewelry and Loans, and Floors Unlimited, and Chain Saw World.

I turned on the rental car's radio and the man on the radio said, "Your gift right now, just twenty dollars a month, could help. Seventy-three more gifts needed. People like you, doing their part. One song left in this challenge. Standing in the gap for those who need it. We here believe in the infallible Word of God. Unchanging principles for changing times."

I drove past something. Then I drove past something else.

*

"There is an awful lot of drugs now in these small towns and big towns both," my uncle Charles said. "You may not know the police shot that boy you all used to play with. Said he was cooking meth down there in his shed. They had him surrounded and he came out alone with his pistol. Found thirty-seven shell casings when it was all done with. What was his name?" But Charles couldn't remember the dead man's name.

"You'll stay with us tonight," my aunt Alice Carol said.

"I have a hotel room near the airport."

"Honey, everything in this town is near the airport."

"I guess I made a foolish decision."

"You've always been foolish."

My aunt was teasing me. She didn't think I was so bad. One Thanksgiving—we were listening to the old boys jaw for hours about hiding up a tree with my grandfather's shotgun in order to shoot a neighbor's brown dog that had killed two of their chickens, and after both barrels were empty there was nothing left but the dog's collar and its tail, which they'd helped the neighbor bury—she turned to me and said, "If you want to be a writer, why don't you go get a pen and paper and write down all these lies?"

✳

Standiford Field was now called Louisville International Airport and the Executive West Hotel was the Crowne Plaza, but Executive Strike & Spare still stood on the other side of Phillips Lane. I walked across the street and shot nine-ball for a couple of lazy hours. It turns out it's like riding a bike—you never forget how, and especially not if you never knew how in the first place.

Overheard at the bar: "He and his friends see this old man take his wallet out at the liquor store, so they know he's got money, and they follow him home. But his wife's there. Now that's two counts. I called him and his mother says, He ain't here. I called back. I said, Santino, I heard you cut your monitor off. You know you got court this Friday? You coming? You know that's another felony? Do not shave your head again, I told him."

"It's funny what order we all remember the salad dressings in."

"My youngest daughter has excellent upper-body strength."

"I sleep very well on the floor."

✳

I took 64 East out of Louisville through the junction. Panels of cars and blown-out tires were scattered in the breakdown lane. I passed Exit 8, the off-ramp to the Southern Baptist Theological Seminary, such as Southern Baptist theology is. The speed limit rose to seventy, and mangled deer, coon, possum, turkeys, and skunks began to appear.

Over the Kentucky River, in Fayette County, I stopped and for three dollars I ate a plate of biscuits and sausage gravy that would almost have fit into a football stadium.

"Here comes Rex. Today's to-do list: raise hell with the waitresses."

"That ain't on his list. That's just normal."

I did not change to the Bert T. Combs Mountain Parkway, which is the way I would have gone fifteen years earlier if I'd been drinking beer with my friend Gary on our way to Red River Gorge before he went crazy and they put him away in Central State for the first time, but not the last.

Gary was a big boy, ugly and pale, with a nose like a peeled potato. I'm not just saying that because my ex-girlfriend slept with him once. We all slept around. She slept with Larry, too, but I don't have anything bad to say about Larry. I myself almost slept with Larry, he was irresistible, a beautiful man. *Gary* and *Larry*—these names have been changed to protect the innocent, but not mine. I am guilty.

Before any of that happened Gary and I were good friends, and we were together in the pro-Martin faction when Lawyer Jack pulled a knife on Big Martin one night in the kitchen of the Highland House and Martin just shrugged and picked up the kitchen table and hit Jack with it.

Gary and I agreed on that dispute and on other important matters, we camped out together, we got high and talked about numerology, and it was in this way that I became important enough to him to lash out at when he fell ill.

"You blue-eyed Jew," he said to me as his mind disappeared. "You dumb piece of fuck. I'm going to stuff six dollars and ninety cents in pennies up your ass and staple it shut."

Six ninety was 138—which was 23 times 6 (the 2 and 3 of 23 multiplied)—times 5 (the 2 and 3 of 23 added). Gary could go on for hours about the significance of these numbers to him. He had infinite bad luck, he would say, because of 138: an unlucky 13 conjoined with the sideways Möbius strip of an 8.

They wheeled him away, strapped to a stretcher.

✳

Gary had written, "Jack looks like your dad! Whew! Happy reading!" in the copy of *On the Road* he gave me for Christmas in 1992. I don't remember if I read it or not. It's about a road.

I didn't have a Dean Moriarty for my long car trip, but I had the man on the car radio. And the man on the radio said: "Pieces of the Divine puzzle will be played out in the coming economic Armageddon. From crisis to consolidation. I want you to pray for me today."

❋

We sang about the Blood Wednesday nights at church suppers, Thursday nights at choir practice, mornings and evenings on Sundays, and every summer at a peacock-ridden revival camp in Alabama.

The old rugged cross, stained with blood so divine. There is a fountain filled with blood. I must needs go on the blood-sprinkled way. He bled, He died to save me. How I love to proclaim it, redeemed by the blood.

They vainly purify themselves, said Heraclitus, *by defiling themselves with blood, just as if one who had stepped into the mud were to wash his feet in mud. Any man who marked him doing thus would deem him mad.*

Our pastor had a method. After his sermon, we sang "Just As I Am" over and over again—without one plea, but that Thy blood was shed for me, and so on. We would sing until someone gave in. We sang all day.

It was the same unrelenting method of the middle-school phys-ed coach who, perceiving that Weak Henry was weak, hit on the technique of making the whole class do extra push-ups until Henry finished his allotted twenty. Henry couldn't make it happen. We did twenty more, thirty more, forty, and, after class, Demetrius and Alonzo beat Henry in the locker room until he peed.

One morning, after an hour of "Just As I Am," my mother shrieked and fell into the aisle. My father helped her stand. His face was strange. The two of them knelt and prayed at the altar. A nice old lady wearing a white gauze eye patch smiled. I waited to see what the people who told me what to do were going to tell me to do next.

※

I played Jesus one year and Judas the next in the Passion play. I taught Vacation Bible School, and visited and sang hymns to the homebound, and, all that rigamarole having been accomplished, I chased the preacher's daughter through the cornfield after Sunday evening services until I caught her.

And my father mowed the field out back of our church. He helped Deacon Jack repaint the sanctuary and he helped Deacon Willy reshingle the roof. He cooked and served at the Wednesday night church suppers and was happy to do it. But he didn't have much time for what he called *churchified* people.

"I find it difficult to believe that the Creator of the universe gives a fuck if I drink a cold beer on a sunny day," my father said. "These people can't say sugar, they just got to say *sucrose*. Meanwhile they don't have no more idea what God wants from me than the man in the moon. It's my own dick I'm talking about, and I can jump up and down on it like a pogo stick if I want to."

※

I thought I was back in Kentucky to write a magazine story about a TV show set in Harlan County. That isn't how things worked out. I wrote this letter instead.

Harlan is not *nowhere*. What you want to do is this: You drive to nowhere, then you turn left. You keep going until page eighty-eight, the last page of the atlas and gazetteer, with its detailed topographical maps, which has apparently been paginated on the assumption that Harlan is the last place you're going to want to go.

In Harlan, in the morning, a woman walked across a restaurant and closed my notebook and said, "You can work all day, honey. Eat your biscuits while they're hot."

And the woman at the hotel's front desk said,

"If you're like those other people, you're going to want a zero balance."

"I guess I am like other people."

"I know all you government men like to keep a zero balance."

I came out of Harlan bewildered on the Kingdom Come Parkway headed back toward Pineville, with its massive floodgates.

The man on the radio said: "I'm going to have a multitude of nations come forth from my loins. And as part of my covenant, You are asking me to mutilate the very part of myself through which You are going to fulfill Your promise. I mean, Abraham, he didn't have the biological insight that we have in our modern medical world, but Abraham knew well where babies come from. And here's God—"

I passed Daniels Mountain and Manito Hill. Out past Tin Can Hollow, I turned south on 25 East. I passed Clear Creek Baptist Bible College and John's Tire Discount and an immense sign that said ARE YOU ADDICTED TO PAIN MEDICATION?

I bore south through Meldrum and Middlesboro (home of the actor Lee Majors, aka Harvey Lee Yeary, aka Colonel Steve Austin, "The Six Million Dollar Man"), all the way to the corner of Virginia, Kentucky, and Tennessee, aka the Cumberland Gap.

Pale-pink-and-white dogwoods and purple wildflowers lined the ascent to Pinnacle Overlook. At the gap, Daniel Boone had penetrated a wall of rock and forest 600 miles long and 150 miles wide. He saw a new world, where all the old mistakes waited to be made again.

When Boone was asked if he had gotten lost in that forest, he said: I can't say as ever I was lost, but I was bewildered once for three days.

※

Back on 25 East, heading north, I drove through crumbling hills past West Roger Hollow and through Corbin into Laurel County. I drove past Magic Vapor Shop and Tri-State Floors. I took 192 East to the Hal Rogers Parkway out past Lick Fork.

Soon I saw a barn I remembered. I saw horses and cows, trailers up on broken cinder blocks, front yards full of table legs and coffee cans. I passed Urban Creek Holiness Church. I passed Jimbo's 4-Lane Tobacco and the Federal Correctional Institution.

At Burning Springs I turned on 472 to head toward Fogertown, where barns had been reclaimed by the land, overgrown with tall trees poking through holes in their roofs. At Muncey Fork was a burnt-down house. Creeping vines were pulling down telephone poles and billboards.

All at once and with no fanfare I passed Cornett Charolais, where I had spent many pleasant Sunday afternoons with old Joe Dale and Dale Junior and Linda and Bessie—pleasant is a pious lie—more like bored, bored, not knowing what all of this would one day mean, what I would one day want to pretend it had all meant.

I wanted it to mean to me what it meant to my father: home and happiness with his foster family. I liked being sent to slop out the hogs after dinner, listening to the rustling in the dark along the fence line. I liked hiking in the rocky hills with my father, seeing that he was calm and pleased, seeing the shale and sandstone and limestone and schist and slate. I liked walking across fields and hearing him holler, "Sookie! Sook calf!"

Apart from those pleasures I had been bored and sullen, reading photocopied pages of *The Antichrist* folded inside *Sports Illustrated*, waiting to escape from that army of hayseeds.

But twenty years later my father's foster mother is dead, as anyone but me might have foreseen, because she was a person and not a tree, and I would eat a photocopier in exchange for two more bowls of her soup beans and cornbread—one for me, and one for my father, to whom it would mean the world made young again.

Instead I name these places. I throw my song

into the mouth of death. I break his teeth. There is no death, there is no hell.

＊

I drove past the old Russell House Grocery, and there was what I wanted to find: the Pleasant Grove Baptist Church, established 1860.

I have seen my father cry three times, and one of those times was in this church, at his foster father's funeral.

The second time I saw my father cry was while he was strangling me. He had said my friends Scott and Allen and Gary were no-good weirdos and long-haired faggots, and I was on the verge of becoming one, too, and that if I didn't act right he was going to cut my hair himself with the lawn mower.

I dared him to, more than a little frightened that he would try it. That was just the sort of thing he was always doing: kicking in a locked door, or pushing around a far-too-young panhandler with a sign that claimed he had been a VIETNAM VETERAN.

"Step around the corner, John Henry," my father said, "I'd like to have a word with this young man in private." He nudged the kid with his boot. "Yes, I do mean you—you dilapidated cocksucker."

And afterward, in the cab of his truck, trembling, beating his fists against the steering wheel, he said, "What's the matter with these people, Johnny? I'm a Vietnam veteran. And just look at me. I'm fine. I'm fine!"

I dared my father to cut my hair, and he picked me up by my throat and smashed me against the wall, then threw me through the doorway into my bedroom and leapt on top of me, and he was strangling me with both hands and shaking me and cursing and shouting at me before he came to his senses and started to cry.

"My family is falling apart," he said, and it was true, I was destroying our family, why couldn't I do as I was told without having impulses and desires of my own.

That is the second time I saw my father cry. The third time is private.

❋

It's not as if my friends *weren't* no-good weirdos. Big Scott had come over earlier that afternoon, and my father had said, "Hey, gorilla." Then: "Scotty, come here, boy, you're hurt."

My father had glimpsed a bloody letter "s" above the collar of Scott's T-shirt. He pulled the collar down and saw the still-bleeding word PUSSY, which Big Scott had cut into his chest with a razor blade moments before sprinting over to show me.

"Who did this to you, boy?" my father said. "You can tell me."

Scott looked at my father.

"I don't believe that," my father said. "No."

✳

I didn't want to write about my father, but I don't seem to have much choice. There is no such thing as a repressed impulse: the inside and the outside are the same side.

What serpent's-tooth-sharp story is this to tell about the man who helped to give me life, who saved my life when I was choking on shish kebab (thereby earning, certain tribesmen might argue, the right to choke me himself), who sacrificed his body at punishing jobs in order that I might have shish kebab to choke on?

Take, eat: this is my body, which is broken for you—and I hope you choke on it.

I visit my father in the Florida Everglades and I see a nice old man. Just this week, he mailed me his sausage-gravy recipe. ("Step Five: Buy helmet, put on, tongue smacking top of mouth may cause injury.")

I am deceived. Where has this nice old man hidden the menacing ogre of my childhood?

His aim was to protect me from the darkness all around us, using the darkness inside himself.

All that darkness had to be *good for something*, didn't it? That was what the darkness was *for*—wasn't it?—not only for tormenting him and, using him as its instrument, everyone he loved?

✳

The man on the radio said, "Four famine scenarios. How to prepare for an economic crisis of Biblical proportions. The salt plan: how to turn adversity into advantage."

"Whence comest thou, Deceiver?" I said. "From going to and fro in the earth, and from walking up and down in it?"

"Be a blessing to others in times of economic turndown. This book will help you get your head straight about what is happening in the world today, and it's very personal and practical at one hundred and forty-two pages."

"Leave me alone," I said to the man on the radio. "That's just the word *God*, the word the conjure man uses to wring hot tears out of the wet rag of your heart. I don't want the word *God*, but the Word of God."

The man on the radio said to me: *I ordained thee a prophet unto the nations.*

I said, "Ah, Lord God, I cannot speak, for I am a child."

But the man on the radio said: *Say not, I am a*

child: for thou shalt go to all that I shall send thee, and whatsoever I command thee thou shalt speak. Behold, I have put my words in thy mouth.

I wept until I had to pull over. God had laid His burning hand on me. If you don't turn the radio off, you can't drive anywhere in this country.

LETTER FROM LEVEL FOUR

Edgar had been a theology student, and a bicycle messenger, and a junk-bonds trader, and now he was working on his master's degree. His new ambition was to become a kindergarten teacher. He felt he needed to have a master's degree in order to teach in a kindergarten.

My neighbor wanted me to spend some time with Edgar. I reminded him of Edgar, he said. We had so much in common. For instance, I had been a janitor, and an exterminator, and a government clerk, and a night watchman, and so on. Neither of us could keep still.

"And you both had fringe-religious child-hoods," my neighbor said. "I'd like to put you two in a room and see what happens."

This is what happened. Edgar and I went to a café. He was a tall, pale kid with dead eyes.

We talked about Las Vegas: he had been there

four times already that year to take photographs, whereas I had seen it glowing from far off in the desert night twenty years before and had driven miles out of my way to avoid it.

After half an hour, Edgar said, "I'm going to tell you a secret. You can't tell anyone. Pretend our meeting never happened. Don't tell my wife."

"Sure," I said. When I got home I wrote down every word.

*

"Last year, this friend of mine dared me to apply to law school. I sent my application, a two-page paper about legal and technical issues in circumcision. I guess the board of admissions didn't approve. They thought it was disrespectful. Their Internet people sent the dogs after me.

"At that time, I was working on a photo project. I had made five separate sites, each ostensibly by a different photographer, each of whom had his own biography. Pseudonyms, prismatic refractions of my identity. Kind of precious.

"Their computer men hacked it all to pieces. They took out the knives. They got in the code and changed it, and they began sending me secret messages. Imagine if you picked up *The New York Times* and your name was in every headline.

"I had to quit Facebook. I couldn't use the Internet anymore—it wasn't safe. They had their agents following my blog under false identities. You have no idea what their technology can do.

"They tore me down and showed me to myself. Not the five false selves of my photo project, but my real self. In the worst light. Did you ever see a film called *The Game*?"

"Is that the one," I said, "where only Michael Douglas is real, and everyone else is a supporting character in an exciting drama made just for him?"

"So you have seen *The Game*?"

"No," I said. "But I heard about it."

"Well, this experience was like *The Game*. Gradually, from hints that my friend let drop, the same friend who had dared me to apply in the first place, I understood that they were hazing me. Incubating me. Preparing me for something greater. The next phase. Teaching me. I shouldn't say who. Winding me up like a toy car with a key. The first sign was that people around me kept talking about cars.

"I shouldn't be telling you any of this. One of them is a MacArthur Fellow—you know, with a genius grant. These Internet kids, they are living in a *Blade Runner* world. They have figured out that most people are—"

"Replicants," I said. "False, synthetic androids. And a lot of them don't even know that they aren't alive."

"That's right," he said. "When my wife got wind of this, she was pretty upset. Two months ago, she asked me to go back into the hospital, and I did, as a favor to her. I love her and I don't want her to worry. The doctors put me back on my antipsychotic medications. And in this way the game was paused."

"Excuse me," I said, and I got up and went to the bathroom. I looked in the mirror, almost always a mistake. I closed my eyes. I was tired of my face.

*

It had been a long time since I'd had a cup of coffee with an insane person. I don't remember much of my own brief stay in the hospital. I remember seeing a sign on the door to my floor that said LEVEL FOUR RISK OF AWOL and thinking, Christ, these people must be nuts.

Two years of parking cars with Martha and Porsche and Ira and Donnie while I sweated out all the drugs I had eaten: that was what brought me back to reality. When Martha was a little girl and asked her father why she had so many freckles, he told her she had been standing behind the cow when it farted. Porsche—one syllable, *porsh*—had a pencil mustache and would try to jump your place in line to get the tip he saw coming to you, maybe a dollar. Ira was a small man but a big drunk, and our cramped staff washroom was perfect for him to be hung over in, since it allowed him to sit on the can while he dangled his tiny head in the sink, retching. Donnie had an exit wound high on his back, between his shoulder blades and just to the right of his spine, where his ex-wife had shot him. Years of my life are in this paragraph: reading the book of Deuteronomy behind a cash register in a parking garage, drinking a six-pack and eating an onion sandwich in my studio apartment. And all of this, they told me, was reality. There are no other worlds than this one. There isn't even this one.

Another man was with me in the bathroom of the café. He was tying his shoe. He had propped his foot, the foot with the lace he was tying, up on the urinal. One end of his untied shoelace hung in the urinal water. I walked out of the bathroom, through the café, straight out the door. I had other things I wanted to do.

I made my way down to the river. The wind wrinkled the water and the sunlight glinted and flickered. Starlings clacked in the grass. Insects hissed and sawed. Whole geese briefly became three-quarters geese as they ducked their heads underwater. Mallards kicked and fidgeted.

✳

"How did it go at the café last week?" my neighbor said.

"Keep that guy away from me," I said.

"I thought he might interest you. Him and his potato phobia."

"We didn't get that far."

My neighbor lit a cigarette. "I found a decapitated rabbit on my porch this morning."

"It's probably a cat."

"It's definitely a rabbit. I haven't seen Edgar for days. Where's his wife? Is he just watching television by himself in there? Do you think I should be worried about him?"

"You should be worried about him whether you see him or not."

My girlfriend ran into Edgar at the café later that week. He wanted to sit with her. "Do I know you?" she said.

"It's me. Edgar. We met at your neighbor's party."

"If you say so."

"Can I sit down?"

"No," she said. "I'm expecting friends."

"Maybe just until they come—"

She reached out with her foot under the table and pulled the chair he was touching closer to her. "No," she said.

"Extreme but effective," I said when she told me her story. It was nice that she had anything to say at all. My relationship with my girlfriend was in one of its off-again phases. Her stock of conversational topics was dwindling. She said the same three or four things over and over again. Was she working something out, was she holding a problem at arm's length? It had happened before. She would take the train to New York to stay with a friend. After a while she would come back, or else one day she wouldn't.

＊

My neighbor had recently rented an office. All he wanted was a place to park his many trucks, but he'd had to take the entire property in order to get control over the lot out back. He hired a man to jackhammer it up and dig it down fresh. He was going to repave it and repaint the spaces.

"I've just about got the front fixed," he said, "and these people won't leave me alone. This is my proposal. The front has a new sign, ferns in the window, and a false wall a quarter of the way back. Behind that, it's pots and pans. In front, it's a desk, and a lamp, and you, looking busy all day. For at least the first eight weeks. To make an impression." He named a price, and I accepted his offer.

My neighbor was not the first person who had paid me to sit around looking the way I did with my blank face, half man and half furniture. As I mentioned, I used to be a night watchman, smoking and listening to the radio.

"It's for my wife that I hire you," the owner of that joint had said. "It's worth it to me, what I pay you, if my wife leaves me alone. Okay? So—night watchman."

"And who watches the place in the daytime?"

He snapped his fingers. "There's nothing to be afraid of in the daytime."

Men like that, business owners, men of property, sized me up at a glance. They assigned me jobs, paid in cash, where I could sit and think my so-called thoughts and look like I was doing nothing, which, as often as not, was exactly what I was doing.

It was nice to put me in a window and ask nothing of me, but I knew that sooner or later Edgar would spy me in his peregrinations as he planned his bright future in the growing field of kindergarten.

It took four days. I was busy throwing a flat-blade screwdriver at the wall to see how many times its sharp end would stick, keeping score in two columns on a yellow legal pad, when Edgar walked past and saw me in the window and stepped in, dragging a small white dog on a leash.

He said, "Did you watch any of those videos I e-mailed you?"

"You can't bring that animal in here. It smells like a skunk shitting bleach."

"Say hello to Particle. I used to call him Wave."

"Potato."

"What?"

"Potato potato."

A siren whined down the street. Edgar's forlorn little dog began to grunt and snuffle. It was trying to howl, but you can't eat scraps under the table for seven years, or forty-nine dog years, and then one day up and decide to let out a howl. All it could manage was a kind of chewy sneeze.

I'd been expecting Edgar: he had e-mailed me a poem he'd written, all eighty-six pages of it. No matter what lazy fun you might be having on a Saturday night—maybe you are performing your assigned exercises, muttering, "I accept myself, I accept myself," gritting your teeth until you worry they will crack; or maybe you are watching a television show in which a researcher injects himself with gonadotropic hormones, followed by an interview with a med-school dropout who claims to have transplanted a monkey's head onto another monkey's body—while you fritter away your precious life in trifles, you can rest easy, knowing that Edgar manfully craps out sodden lumps of poetry, shaking his bathroom with the thunder of his spirit. What had he eaten for dinner? His poem stank in my nostrils.

Edgar said, "What about that thing I sent you to read?"

I had purchased an emergency potato and put it in my top desk drawer, and when he saw it in my hand he got moving in a hurry—or perhaps it was my cologne, Air of Menace. Down the road he went. I waited until the coast was clear and I took my break.

I smoked a cigar by the river in the heat and the glassy stillness. A cormorant found a fish. A night heron trailed his legs behind him as he flew. A cloud of gnats danced frantically in the hot light. Small white butterflies fought, or teased one another, or courted: I didn't have enough information to understand their relationships. All I was good for that year was watching waterbirds.

*

Edgar is not his real name, by the way. His real name is Martin.

His loneliness was terrifying to me. It presented me with a struggle between abstract fellow feeling, morality, large-mindedness, *Have mercy on a sinner like yourself*—none of them my strong suit—between those high ideals on the one hand, and fidelity to felt experience on the other: for a nickel I would proctologize him with a straight razor, dear God, please let him die.

He didn't deserve it. Edgar was a sensitive, odd, unhappy man who had taken far too many drugs and had not yet sweated them out, that was all. I had known others like him. This much I understood, and I wanted my understanding to cancel him, to eliminate him, like a proof or a problem in a child's geometry homework. The problem has been solved, let us move on.

But the world is not my private fiefdom, it is our common property. One morning I spotted Edgar at the grocery store, stumbling, stunned. I had just finished working out at the YMCA and was still sweating, pushing my cart full of blackberries, cantaloupe, bunches of arugula, tomato juice, and there stood Edgar, a man like me.

He seemed upset to encounter me, and why not. Edgar, in the dairy aisle, saw me seeing him and he winced, he froze, he was afraid even to wave—or was it my own fear it seemed I saw myself seeing in him? He, too, had wanted a new friend. It was not entirely his fault that he was a fool.

∗

Pretty soon my girlfriend wasn't speaking to me. She left town. Fine. When would she be back? When she came back. That's fine. I picked up a two-piece fried-chicken box with macaroni and cheese and black-eyed peas, and I settled in to watch television all night by myself. I watched *Solo Boxeo* on Univision. I watched *The Game*.

The Game is 128 minutes long, thirty-eight minutes longer than a movie should be. It is the story of Nicholas Van Orton's forty-eighth birthday.

Nick's brother, Conrad, connects him to CRS, an outfit that designs a persecution experience for him: "the game."

It soon becomes difficult for Nicholas to distinguish the texture of life itself from the design of the game. Faced with a pedestrian having a heart attack on the sidewalk, he asks, "How do we know he's real?"

He kills his brother, then, baffled and grief-stricken, throws himself from the roof of a skyscraper—but he falls onto an inflated pillow placed specially to catch him. The game is over! His brother is alive! And all of his friends are waiting for him at his birthday party!

My notes follow.

12 min 06 sec	Outlandish, degrading, crass stupidity. Crimes against the human mind.
48 min 35 sec	Pure corn.
01 hr 05 min	"I have a gun." WHAT TRASH.
01 hr 24 min	Not only is it not credible, but the extent of its implausibility is itself beyond belief.
01 hr 54 min	Dirt, boredom, filth, lies.

✳

An overeducated dope like Edgar, a former semi-
narian and a drug casualty, had never had a chance,
not from the moment the actor at the twenty-
three-minute mark said, "You want to know what
it is? What it's all about? John, chapter nine, verse
twenty-five—whereas once I was blind, now I
can see."

I remembered, with atypical clarity, watching
Clint Eastwood as Dirty Harry Callahan in *The
Dead Pool* in a motel in Phoenix, or was it Tucson,
or possibly Flagstaff, explaining to a bored girl that
the movie's obligatory car chase, in which a bomb-
equipped remote-control car pursues the hero, was
a brilliant parody of the genre's tired conventions,
but it was only the drugs I had taken performing
their predictable alchemy of transmuting two hours
of television into a lecture.

"You peed on me again last night while you
were asleep," the girl said. "Are you sure you're
okay?"

John 9:32—"Since the world began was it not
heard that any man opened the eyes of one that was
born blind." Whereas I was blind, now I am still as
blind as I ever was, but alas, I have become con-
vinced that I can see.

I was impatient to discuss this and other topics
with Edgar. I crouched in the damp bushes in front
of his porch, waiting for him to return from his
Wednesday-night graduate seminar. His little dog

barked for two or three minutes before giving up its feeble pretense of guarding the perimeter. I knew the students often went out together for a drink after class but my knees and hips were strong, my hamstrings and lower back were flexible, I could wait all night in the dark. I was going to explain everything. I wanted to surprise him.

LETTER FROM DEVILS TOWER

When he opened his pay envelope and saw that Ermin, the bakery's owner, had shorted him for the second time in a month, he wrote a note. "You owe me eight hundred dollars," the note said. "I finished my route. I took the van and sold it. I'll bring you the balance Monday morning."

He stapled his note to the screen door. He got back in the maroon van full of dusty trays and pulled out of the lot across the street from the bakery. He headed east on Oak Street and turned left on Floyd, and at Saint Catherine he took the on-ramp for I-65 North.

It wasn't a bad job, even if it was rough on his knee. He enjoyed driving, with its seductive illusion of getting somewhere, as if motion and progress were identical. He liked to look at maps: X marks the spot, you are no longer here.

He often dreamt of driving clear across the

country. Those double yellow lines kept coming at him. "I notice that in this fantasy you are alone," a caseworker had once told him, and it was as if she had said, *I notice that your hair is hair-colored.*

※

For a long time he had been the kind of person who didn't have a cell phone. But one evening, after dinner, his wife had become enraged and had said, When are you going to get a cell phone, and he had said, I thought maybe it would be simpler to have a tracking device installed in my cervical spine, and his wife had said, For Christ's sake, will you just grow up and get a cell phone already, and now he was no longer the kind of person who didn't have a cell phone.

He crossed over the Ohio River into southern Indiana. There was nothing to stop him from throwing it out the window: his old life through a figurative window, his phone through an actual van window, everything. What would Jesus do, Jesus didn't have a cell phone.

He struck the phone on the knob of the gearshift several times, hard, until its screen cracked, *chikt.* He rolled down his window and threw the phone out of the van. Now he was that kind of person.

He pulled over and walked back and waited for a pause in the traffic and got the phone. It was ringing.

"Margaret tells me you won't be coming home this weekend," his wife said.

That Margaret, he thought. "How is Margaret?" he said.

"I don't know who you think you're fooling."

"Not even myself."

"Why won't you just admit what you're up to?"

"I don't know that a man can be asked to admit what he has never taken the trouble to hide. If you see my point."

"I do see it," she said. "If you look to the left and right of my nose, you will observe my eyes, which I use for seeing. But I understand if you have to fuck her. To say goodbye. I understand if you have to fuck her to say goodbye."

"I don't want to fuck her goodbye," he said.

"Just don't fuck me on the same day," his wife said. "If you have to fuck her, I understand."

＊

Karen was wearing a pale-green sweater even though it wasn't cold. She had cut her hair short again. He liked it long, he liked it short.

Once, when her hair was short and she had sent him a photo of it on the cell phone, he had cut his off, too, and stood in front of the bathroom mirror at home and pretended to be her.

"What are you doing?" his wife had said, and he had said, "What do you think I'm doing?"

✳

"You drive a van?" Karen said.

"Never mind. What time do you get off work?"

"How does right now suit you?" She got in. "This van smells like a biscuit. I guess you remember I don't go all the way on the first date."

"I don't know if I go all the way at all anymore."

"We'll see," she said. "You look terrible."

She'd gone to school for years to study *library science*. He didn't see how it could be so complicated. It seemed like a hoax.

"Where are we headed?"

"Kingman," he said. "Barstow. San Bernardino."

She drummed her fingers on the dashboard, *thrup.* "Then it's going to be a while."

"With my arm hanging out the window. And by the third day, your arm is so sunburned that you have to roll your sleeve back down. That's what America means to me."

"Here. Hold this." She pushed her purse at him. He was being tested for subservience. He did not move.

"Be careful," she said. "Don't touch it. You might break out in little purses and purse yourself to death."

He felt his headache coming on and took three tiny white pills. Karen turned the radio on and off and said, "Let's play a game. Each of us will tell something he doesn't like about the other person. I'll go first. You don't have a headache yet, you can't be sure you're going to get your headache, but you take a pill. It's wasteful, showing that you are a bad steward of your resources. It's impatient, anxious, panicked, I might even say cowardly. Your turn."

＊

His phone rang. "Can it possibly be true," Margaret said on the other end of the line, "that you have blocked both of Ermin's phones? You got shit jammed up back here. I am not delivering no dinner rolls on a bicycle."

"It's not that I'm not interested in your personal problems, Margaret. It's that, like any other self-respecting psychiatric caregiver, I charge two hundred and fifty dollars an hour to listen to them. That's more than four dollars per minute."

"Tell me just one thing. Where are you?"

"Monaco. Antarctica. Beautiful downtown Samarkand."

"Send me a postcard, baby," Margaret said.

＊

"Why don't we stop and get something to eat?" Karen said. "You're too skinny. You look like an anteater."

He was looking at her but he couldn't hear her. He was listening to the other people in the diner. "I feel as if you're trying to control my every thought," the woman at the table to his left said to the man with her, almost certainly her husband.

"Try to focus," Karen said. "I'm going to call my sister."

He thought he was staring into blank space, but space was not blank. Space was as full of people and objects as ever. He was staring at steak and poached eggs with Cholula sauce, wheat toast. He shifted his weight on the lumpy red vinyl of his seat.

He was staring at the waitress. "Do you want something else?" the waitress said.

"What do Americans want?" he said. "Read any newspaper. We want to kill each other. It's not hard to understand."

"I'll bring your check," the waitress said.

Karen came back and sat down. Now that she had his attention, she didn't want it.

She said, "There's not much more to tell. My cousin Calvin? He dressed up like a circus clown and took a kitchen knife and robbed a woman out in front of a strip-mall jewelry store. And our spaniel died. Sarah has bad dreams about it. She says the dog comes back and speaks to her."

"What does the dog say?"

"Please don't ask me questions like that."

"I knew a man who said he could talk to the spirits of dead animals."

"What kinds of animals?"

"It was a hamster in the story he told me. His college-age son came back over the break with a pet hamster. The boy takes off and the father is supervising the hamster. He doesn't like to see a living thing in a metal cage, he says. He lets it out to run around on the floor in the daytime. At night he puts it back in the cage. One morning, he sees that the hamster has broken its jaw, almost broken it off, trying to gnaw through the metal bars. It dies. And in his dreams the dead hamster explains to him from the spirit realm that he had shown it freedom, and it loved freedom too much to stay in the cage."

"It's a nice story about freedom. My favorite part is how it changes 'I killed my son's hamster' into 'I have magical powers.'"

"I want hamster freedom."

"You are talking about hamster death," she said. "You ought to try being a woman sometime. You'd learn a lot."

"Will you look at this jerk?" he said, gesturing to a nearby table, half hoping to start an argument with her or with someone else, it didn't matter. "Playing with his mashed potatoes. Like Richard Dreyfuss in *Close Encounters of the Third Kind*."

"That movie is better than people say."

"What people?"

"It's a movie about faith. They're staring into the sky, saying, 'Oh my God.' Waiting for the angel Gabriel, who stands in the presence of God, to show them glad tidings. Or for Christ Himself to knock them flat on the road to Damascus."

"They would be," he said. "Waiting. What point is there waiting for something like that to happen. When you think of everything you yourself could get done."

"And you think because there's no point to wanting what you want, you just aren't going to want it anymore."

"I am gnawing through the bars of my cage."

"You didn't pay much attention to your friend's story," Karen said. "Go on and tell yourself you can bite your way to freedom with your mighty mouth. I see your mouth moving. You think you're biting, but you're just talking. I see the cage. The cage is still there."

Richard Dreyfuss had not even looked at them. He was far away, in a Wyoming of his mind.

*

The little girl with her hair in two braids who seemed to run the motel handed him a coupon for painkillers. The coupon had been cut out neatly from a larger sheet of newsprint and dotted lines ran along its edge. "Am I that ugly?" he said. She cocked her head, studying his eyes, then went into a back room and came out with the painkillers themselves.

"You do not have to buy them," she said.

His whole life, the drugs that killed pain and the drugs that had caused it, the present wife and the disappeared ex-wife gone off to North Africa somewhere, all of it had begun years ago as a kind of performance art. Who was he fooling? Not even himself. Some nights he stared at the ceiling and wished he had snapped out of it and gotten a sex-reassignment surgery, or something else contemporary. Instead he had made a face and it had stuck this way.

The motel walls were striped. The upholstery was striped, the bedclothes were striped. The room was full of lamps with their cords.

In bed, the procedure was as had long ago been established. Nothing could excite her except being ignored.

If he yawned and watched television, or pretended to watch television, she came, or pretended to be able to keep coming, until she had to vomit, or pretended to vomit. She locked the bathroom door behind her. The entire production was less convincing than he remembered.

"Do you know the other two kinds of close encounters?" he said to the bathroom door. The glass or plastic doorknob was faceted, as if it were a cut gem. "The first is when you catch a glimpse. The second kind is crop circles, physical evidence. What are you doing in there?"

"I'm praying on my knees to Jesus," the bathroom door said. "What we just did was wrong."

"All right."

"You can leave me here. My sister will pick me up."

"Imagine that," he said. He slept in the van, in the parking lot, and woke with a neck ache. He looked in the rearview mirror. There are visions a man can only tolerate in a mirror. To see them face-to-face turns him to stone.

※

White lines and yellow lines. Green grass and yellow grass. Far-off hills. Mile markers. Telephone poles standing in line, waiting for what. He was ripping southward on the interstate just as fast as the other cars could get out of his way, in a van he didn't own. He had driven this stretch of highway all his life. It was haunted. He saw things he knew weren't there. He wanted to close his eyes.

He was glad he still had his phone. Someone, somewhere, might call him and have something useful to tell him. He considered that unlikely possibility for half an hour. He rolled down the window and threw his phone out of it.

He pulled the van over to the shoulder and sat there, thinking and making decisions, reminding himself that he had for the most part freely chosen what at other times he claimed had been forced on him.

He walked back toward his phone. His knee gave out as he bent to pick it up. On the road the cars roared past him, almost close enough to touch, on their ways to all the places they thought they were going. He waited there, on his knees.

LETTER FROM THE PRIMAL HORDE

I entered psychoanalysis because I felt I was becoming intolerable to the people around me. I loved
them, and they deserved better.

After five years, my analyst suggested that
I attend a residential group-relations conference,
thinking the experience might shed some new light
on my old problems.

✳

What is group relations? If your job involves attend-
ing meetings, then you know most meetings are a
waste of time. We sense that what we are talking
about cannot be what we are actually talking about,
because, if it were, events would occur in a different
order, and the tone or feeling would be different, and
so on. Something else is happening to us, through us,
and among us.

Now imagine a professional meeting with no
pseudo-unifying pseudo-topic, where the meeting's

topic is the meeting itself: the New England Motor Press Association, but shorn of New England, motors, and the press. Nothing remains but the association, the something else, the group, the collective, if it does remain: a shrewdness of apes, a gang of turkeys, a nest of vipers.

"The Group Relations Conference," says the Web site of the A. K. Rice Institute for the Study of Social Systems, "is an intensive participatory process that provides participants the opportunity to study their own behavior as it happens in real time without the distractions of everyday social niceties and workplace pressures and protocols."

And they have to say something corporate-klutzy-jargony like that, don't they, because if they were to come right out and say, "You are cordially invited to have your individual ego reduced to molten slag in the hell-furnace of our collective unconscious," no one would sign up.

What does such a conference reveal, if not the something else that is not the people at the meeting: the something else that is not "me," but conspires to act through "me," then disowns me and claims, in a bizarre act of half-justice, that I am to be held responsible for both its actions and my own.

—The good that I would I do not; but the evil which I would not, that I do.

—Really? Whose unconscious is it, anyway?

—Maybe the answer to that question is more complex than it appears.

At first I refused to go. A year later, I attempted to enroll, but there were no places open. Another year passed. I packed my suitcase and boarded the commuter rail.

❋

"You did not indicate your career when you registered for the conference," said the wide-eyed man at the front desk.

"You noticed that?" I said.

Silence.

"There's a line here"—he waved the paper at me—"for you to say what profession you're in."

"I see that."

Silence.

"But you did not fill it out."

"That's correct."

"We use that information to organize your debriefing groups."

"Is that right?"

Silence.

"I'm a writer," I said. It is almost always an error to admit this, and possibly an error ever to say or to write anything at all.

Many attendees were made ill at ease by the discovery of a writer in their midst. Thirty-six psychiatrists, chaplains, social workers, counselors, nurses, and others in the caring professions had been sent by their respective employers to investigate authority and institutional life by improvising an institution and analyzing it, if they could—or, as things turned out, by failing to improvise such an institution, and by failing to analyze that failure.

Thirty-six white-collar professionals and one writer, devoted to following his frequent errors wherever they might lead him.

Many people hate writers. As the judge snarled at Brodsky, "Who has recognized you as a poet? Who has enrolled you in the ranks of poets?" It's true that something has gone wrong in a family or a group that gives birth to a writer, a person whose role is to escape and tell the tale. But the hatred at the conference had a particular flavor.

What would Freud have amounted to without Sophocles or Shakespeare, without Dostoyevsky or even Jensen? Psychoanalysts and writers might seem to be natural allies, covering the same territory. Now I understand that psychoanalysts and writers are natural enemies precisely because they cover the same territory. Only a child would be surprised.

Don't worry, I changed your name. I made it all up. There is no such thing as a door or a chair. Psychoanalysis does not exist.

✳

It is not much of an exaggeration to say that the staff locked us in and left us to work it all out for ourselves.

"I welcome you to the conference," said the director at our first meeting. He sat down among the other consultants. There was a long silence.

"What now?" said Tommy.

"Yes," said the director. "What now?"

I had read the brochure: "The consultant confronts the group by drawing attention to group behavior. This is done by means of description, process observation, thematic development, and other interventions, some of which are designed to shock the group into awareness of what is happening." What this meant in practice was that our consultants rarely intervened, and for the most part served as silent projection magnets, embodiments of authority for us to pretend not to resent.

Sometimes thirty-seven of us were seated in a gray room: this was the "large group." At other times we were taken to separate rooms in groups of ten or so: a "small group." Ten people in a room, seventy-five minutes. Thirty-seven people in a room, seventy-five minutes. Self-forming groups in rooms of our choosing, seventy-five minutes. Five of these meetings per day. No other rules.

Our regression was swift. It is incorrect to use the word "I" when describing mass-hysterical events. My feelings were not special or unique. They were not even mine.

✳

"I don't have an image for this conference," Tommy said.

"What does that mean?" said Vicki.

"I don't know your names. Tell me your names," said Tommy.

"I know your name," said Eric. "I know everyone's name."

"We told each other our names yesterday," Vicki said.

"Maybe the name is not the name," said our consultant.

We went around the small group and said our names again. Tommy, Samantha, Vicki, Jennifer, Martin, Eric, Renata, Federico, and Tina.

"My name is Ronald," I said.

"Hello, Ronald," said Tommy. "I am Tommy. Pleased to meet you."

"His name is not Ronald," Vicki said.

"That's enough about the names for now," I said. "Five minutes before this meeting, I threw up my breakfast into the sink in my room. Isn't anyone else here as nervous as I am?"

"Why did you choose to throw up alone in your

room?" said our consultant. "Don't you feel you can throw up here in our group?"

"I threw up scrambled eggs and two cups of coffee mixed with the juices of my stomach. Not metaphorical undigested emotions. Yellow-and-brown vomit."

"Thanks for the image," said Vicki.

"I know I talk a lot," said Tommy. "I take up too much space in our small group. I wish someone would tell me to shut up."

"Okay. Shut up," said Samantha.

"Shut up," said Tina.

"Shut up, Tommy," said Eric.

"Please shut up," said Vicki.

"How can you speak to me like this?" Tommy said.

※

Back to the large group.

"Some group members may still not be aware that there is a writer present. When is management going to address my concerns about confidentiality?" said Barry, who would soon write and publish his own report of our conference on his Web site.

"I feel ashamed," said Rhonda.

"So far, I have learned one thing at this conference," said Dora, "and it is that Americans say hello by saying *Go fuck yourself.*"

"I've never understood the expression *Go fuck yourself*," said Sean.

"I'm cold," said Karen.

"I have a nodule in my chest," said Eric. "It's my companion. I have a companion."

"I feel fear," said Anna.

"I am also afraid," said Jane.

"I feel the men in the group are being submissive," Brian said.

"I'm taking a bold stand against reductive gender binaries," said Patricia.

"I have so much to contribute," said Travis, "but no one will give me a chance."

"Tell us, Travis. Tell us what you have to say," said Margaret.

"Uh," said Travis. "Okay. Uh. Uh."

"Everything everyone says here sounds like a pickup line," Malik said.

"Pickup lines work," said Pilar. "Trust me."

"I'm bored," said Tina.

"The group appears to be attempting to ignore and deny its aggression," said the conference director.

"I am aware of the group's aggressive feelings," I said. "For example, I would like to kill you."

❋

By the thirtieth time Eric explained to the large group that "it's all about respect," it had become clear to me that what he meant was, *Everyone else must shut up when I am talking*, something I have heard many three-year-olds say, or scream.

I shared this interpretation with the group, and Eric promptly had a heart attack. But it was not a real heart attack, not even a little, not at all. Eric was taken by ambulance to a local hospital and was swiftly returned to us, resurrected, in perfect health, if *health* is the word for a strategy of illness-as-leadership or weakness-as-strength.

A. K. Rice himself pointed out "how the group uses individuals to express its own emotions, how it exploits some members so that others can absolve themselves from the responsibility for such expression." Several people thanked me for saying what they themselves had not wished to say to or about Eric.

A man told me, "You are our strongest advocate for reality," and a woman said, "I hope you know how grateful we all are to you for speaking out."

"It's like you can read my mind," another woman said.

It was odd to be told that I was "the real, responsible parent" at the exact moment when I felt as if I were Norman Bates from *Psycho*—but Norman is his own parent, isn't he.

✳

This was not my first excursion into the primitive substrata of human consciousness. I was just doing it without hallucinogens for a change.

As night fell on the second day of the conference, I felt I had already acquired an adequate grasp of the basic concepts of *Experiences in Groups*, W. R. Bion's brilliant study of "the individual [as] a group animal at war, not simply with the group, but with himself for being a group animal and with those aspects of his personality that constitute his 'groupishness,' " and I was not looking forward to four more days of experiences in groups.

I had understood yet again, and more thoroughly than ever, how and why I have chosen my line of work (we might call it *the emotion-recollected-in-tranquillity racket*), in which I spend one-third of my time having experiences in groups and the other two-thirds sitting alone in a room, thinking about what went wrong.

"Group mentality," writes Bion, "is the unanimous expression of the will of the group, contributed to by the individual in ways of which he is unaware, influencing him disagreeably whenever he thinks or behaves in a manner at variance with the basic assumptions."

Bion's basic assumptions are *dependency*, in which a group unites to pretend its impotence in order to rely on an imagined omnipotent leader; *fight-*

flight, in which a group derives unity from either attacking or fleeing from an identified enemy; and *pairing*, a kind of predependency in which a group demotes itself to helpless expectation by focusing on two members and waiting for the birth of their messiah-child.

We had waited for the conference director to tell us what to do next, as if we weren't free to do just as we pleased. We had fought Eric—I had, on behalf of the group—and he had obligingly fled to the hospital.

My private apartment on campus contained two tiny quarter-beds that I pushed together to form a single half-bed, and a tiny black chairlike object unsuitable for sitting on, and a tiny sink for me to throw up in. Each night I locked my door and jammed the chairlike object against it and wore noise-canceling headphones and sat on the bed-like objects, thinking about what had gone wrong that day.

Across the hall from me was a distinguished sort of person with plenty of exotic stories to share. We ate lunch together. He had attended twelve of these conferences, he told me.

At three the next morning, this grown man stood undressed in the hallway, hammering on the unlocked door of his apartment. He knocked on my door for a while, too.

"Help me," he said. "I'm naked. Let me come in your bedroom."

"Listen to the words you are saying," I told him through the door. "What words did you just say?"

"Help me. Help me."

"Yes, those are some of the words you said."

"Help me."

In the end, a woman woke up and went out in the hall and showed him how to operate a door-knob. You turn it from side to side.

✳

Freud, in "Creative Writers and Day-Dreaming":

> There is one very marked characteristic in the production of these writers which must strike us all: they all have a hero who is the center of interest, for whom the author tries to win our sympathy by every possible means . . . His Majesty the Ego, the hero of all day-dreams and all novels . . .
>
> The other people in the story are sharply divided into good and bad, with complete disregard of the manifold variety in the traits of real human beings; the "good" ones are those who help the ego in its character of hero, while the "bad" are his enemies and rivals.

LETTER FROM THE PRIMAL HORDE

✳

The problem with telling the story of the conference from a single character's point of view is that
this obscures the major insight that group relations
has to offer.

Most readers will be familiar with the experience of watching a certain kind of movie and understanding that, just as a dreamer is all of the
characters in his dream, so, too, Dutch is the hated
Predator, Ripley is the Alien Queen, the good archaeologist Indiana Jones is the bad archaeologist
Belloq, the red-blooded Flash Gordon is the anemic
Ming the Merciless, and so on.

These are stories of disowning parts of the self,
projecting unwanted traits into an enemy, and con-
templating the unwanted traits at a safe distance—
typically, in a climactic confrontation, the "hero"
denies his essential identity with the "villain" by
destroying these traits along with the enemy who
contains them.

At a group-relations conference, it is the *group*
that is the "hero"—or the patient. My name was
Legion, for we were many; "I" was large, "I" contained multitudes. The most fictional part of this
story is the nonplural "I" that narrates it.

Scenes from previous pages ought to be rewrit-
ten. But how?

"I feel shame," said the primal horde.

"I feel fear," said the primal horde.

"I would like to kill you," the primal horde said.

"I know your name," the primal horde said. "I know everyone's name."

*

The group mind presents certain problems. Leave aside that His Majesty the Ego has been demoted from a star to just another flicker of light in a constellation, a mere organ in a larger social organism. *There is nothing outside the group.* Where can you project all of your disowned traits now?

I wasn't surrounded by assholes. I was trapped inside of one.

*

On the third day of the conference, I cut class. What were they going to do—arrest me?

Angry, lonely, tired, and frightened, I spent an afternoon in the woods on campus. I hiked until the trees ended. I had been walking down a two-lane country road for some time when a stranger with a short gray beard pulled his truck over and offered me a lift to the next town.

As strangers sometimes will, we took advantage of the moment to tell each other everything we knew. He told me disturbing secrets about his parents. I told him I was an escapee from a PSYOPS experiment.

"You're not serious."

"More or less." I gave him some examples.

"That is the most amphetaminized shit I have ever heard. You need a drink."

"I haven't had a drink in ten years."

"That could be your problem right there."

"In a manner of speaking."

He pulled over at a liquor store. "You sure you don't want anything?"

"I am sure I want something that I had better not have."

He drove me back to the campus. There I was taken to a wood-paneled office with two consultants and a whiteboard on a folding stand, or is it a wipeboard, it's never been clear to me what people call that thing.

"I still don't understand. You went outside?"

"These people keep telling me I am saying their thoughts for them."

"I'm sure that is true," one of the consultants said, pulling his chair closer to mine. "Never mind this game now. I'm talking to you seriously, man to man. Do not walk away from here filled up with everybody else's shit, full of other people's feelings. You aren't doing them any favors. That's their shit.

Leave their shit here, for them to deal with. I'm warning you."

But it was no use warning the child who had once put his hand on the grill because he had wanted to know how it felt to be a hamburger.

※

When someone leaves a group-relations conference early, it's called a *casualty*. Who dies? The one who leaves, or the group that is left behind?

By electing a single member to contain disowned psychotic anxieties and extruding that member, the group both "kills" him and dismembers itself.

Before lunch on the fourth day, during seventy-five minutes in the large group, I became uneasy about the group's enforcement of Tommy's prolonged silence. His wish to be told to shut up had been cruelly granted: he had not spoken for more than twenty-four hours.

He was seated on the floor outside our circle. It had become impossible not to see that we were no longer seeing him.

All of the people seated behind the director had their legs crossed, their arms crossed, hands over their mouths. It was extraordinary. They were a wall of defense—defending whom, from what? And behind them, behind that wall, on the floor, with his back to us and ours to him, sat the sullen, silenced Tommy.

I wanted Tommy out of quarantine. I wanted whatever we had put inside him and walled off and banished from our consciousness to be returned to us at once, for his sake and for the sake of the group.

I tried to explain this, but I opened my mouth and was surprised to find that I was incoherent.

＊

And the Lord said, Behold, the people *is* one, and they have all one language; and this they begin to do: and now nothing will be restrained from them, which they have imagined to do. Go to, let us go down, and there confound their language, that they may not understand one another's speech.

＊

After that meeting I locked myself in my campus apartment, in the dark, but my room wasn't dark enough. I got into the closet and closed its door. That wasn't dark enough, either. I began to tie a shirt around my neck.

I am in a room in the dark, I thought, inside a larger locked room in the dark, strangling myself. These are the actions of a disturbed person.

THE CORRESPONDENCE

It was my punishment for refusing to forget Tommy: his role of group "demon" had been reassigned to me, as Pazuzu leaps from Regan to Father Karras in *The Exorcist*.

I threw my suitcase out a window and jumped out after it. Any landing you can walk away from is a good one. I limped to the nearest town and hired a car.

※

When I got home, I ripped paintings and photographs off my walls, shouting, "Demons, I cast you out," and threw armloads of framed pictures out my front door, but then I had to sweep up all that broken glass, and while I was sweeping I began to vomit, and now I was sweeping both broken glass and vomit, not the most sweepable of mixtures, and I continued to attempt to clean up the mess while— honesty requires this admission—at the same time I continued, with my ceaseless vomiting, to create that same mess, and soon I had to get three antipsychotic prescriptions to calm down. It took me five months to calm down. Otherwise I suffered no adverse effects.